The practice of creating a modern business

Contents

Chapter 1. Before the start of business 4
    Problem № 1. Employment 5
    Problem № 2. Lack of money 7
    Problem № 3. Responsibility 7
    Problem № 4. Creating the first source of income 7
    Problem № 5. Your boss is a piece of shit 8
    Problem № 6. There's no business teaching at the university 9
    Problem № 7. "Test it out"/ "Having your own business is in fashion" 9
    What should you be prepared for? 9
    1. Relatives 10
    2. Absolute impropriety of knowledge 10
    3. Information is evil. 11
    4. Doubt – action 11
    5. The dips. 12
    Conclusions: 12
    Tasks: 12

Chapter 2. Goals. How to choose a business that will survive in the future? 13
    Introduction to the goals 14
    Questions before we start. 15
    Financial calculation. 16
    Motivation. 18
    When to quit the business? 19
    Seven steps to setting business goals 19
    Lifestyle 22
    Preparing for the business creation – drawing a portrait of your surroundings. 22
    Conclusions: 23
    Tasks: 23

Chapter 3. Juridical Issues 24
    Revenue service 24
    What do I choose – SP or LLC? 24
    What to do with inspections? 24
    "Shakedown" and "protection" 25
    How to close the deal without being a legal entity? 25
    Conclusions: 26
    Tasks: 26

Chapter 4. What is business? Defining some terms before the start. 27

What is business?..27
Types of business...28
"Odessa-style business". 5 easy ways for partisans to quickly create a business "from scratch"...29
Business plan. Myth or Reality?..35
Conclusions: 35
Tasks:..35

Chapter 5. Finding the niche..37
How to formulate your niche?..37
Portrait of the target audience or "for whom is our niche?"................................38
Two simple tools for choosing a niche on the Internet..40
Evaluating flow of competitors 43
Choosing a niche from offline to online and vice versa. 43
Search for suppliers. 44
How to work with suppliers, having no money to purchase a product?............45
Criteria for a successful niche. 45
Conclusions: 46
Tasks:..46

Chapter 6. Launching the traffic and advertising your business 48
Qualitative incoming stream (QIS)...48
How to get a QIS? 48
How to make selling ads? Basic copywriting..49
PPHS..53
What to advertise? "Frontend" and "backend"..55
Direct mail 57
Partnership programs 61
Internet advertising 61
Announcements boards..61
Internet advertising: banners, teasers..63
Internet advertising: YD and GA. Contextual advertising 64
Internet advertising: SMM, VK, FB 68
A few words from a partisan. 71
Conclusions: 72
Tasks:..72

Chapter 7. Conversion and Convertors...74
What is a "conversion"? 74
Purpose of the website..75
Template scheme of the selling "landing page" 76
Home page..78

"Catalog" section and product page. 81
Social Networks – creating the sales platform 83
Convertor: seller - phone. 84
Convertor: seller - shop. 87
Convertor: store - merchandising 88
Convertor: shop - price tag 90
Convertor – office...91
Conclusions: 92
Tasks:..93

Chapter 8: The average check 94
How to set the price? 94
How to build the product matrix - Up / Down / Cross Sales..............................95
Up / Down / Cross Sale. 96
Announced bonuses. Sales magnets. 98
Bundles (sets). 98
How to control the average check. 99

Chapter 9. Clients 100
Four types of clients 100
Four types of clients – "Middleman" - professional...100
Four types of clients – "Urgent" 101
Four types of clients - VIP..101
9.5 One-time / regular customers 101
The Matrix of customers...102
Customer database. 103
The first customers. 104
Map of the territory...104
Cold and warm customers 105
Attracting clients on a long term basis. 105
Conclusions: 108
Tasks:..108

Chapter 10. Automation of business..109
Types of business processes 109
The structure of business processes 109
Accounting..110
Scripts and bureaucracy 111
"Semi-automatic" 111
Automatic systems..112
Financial Management 112
Conclusions: 115

Tasks: 115
Afterword: 116

Chapter 1. Before the start of business

In this chapter, you will discover why people come in business. What is it that leads them to building up the business? Which happenings and changes in their lives and attitude motivate them to think about self-employment?

According to statistical indexes people, who decide to start up their own business, are usually driven by seven main causes:

1. Quitting your job.
2. Lack of money.
3. Responsibility.
4. Perspective of the lack of money.
5. The Boss.
6. New experience or knowledge.
7. "Try something new" / "It's a trend"

Look at this list carefully and ask yourself: why have YOU decided to do this now? HOW do you imagine your life in the future? WHY do you even want to start your own business?

I understand it perfectly: if you had been all arranged, you wouldn't have ever opened this book. Starting you own business – a step, which can change everything in your life. Although to start moving, you have to know where you want to get.

This book is a practical guide for those, who want to run their own business. To make this decision demands taking a huge responsibility, but you trust me – it's fully worth it! By reading this book, you will change your life.

To understand the mechanism of starting your own business, let's discuss why do people even bother trying.

Problem № 1. Employment

Each one of us has the first thing to begin – get a job in someone else's company. Because now we are studying the general principle, the field doesn't matter – you can work as an ordinary barber or a regular dancer of ballet troupe. But in time, the man that got a job, growth to a certain level and become a specialist in his profession. By that time, his labor is paid higher, he is more appreciated, more demanded. Seems, what else is needed? Your career is successful!

However, steadily a tipping point comes in consciousness of this man and he understands that his value as a specialist is much higher than the cost of goods he's getting by working as an employee. As the result, he begins to consider the self-employment.

The logic of this man is simple: if he could succeed in his career, he can easily succeed in starting his own business and get much more income! It really turns out for some of them – former employees simply create some sort of a "clone" of their previous working place.

Therefore, the first problem, which pushes the man into creating his own company – he doesn't like working for someone else. People desire freedom, they want to earn as much as they truly deserve!

If you fall into this category, then this book will be invaluably helpful for you – it helps hired workers to start up a business.

The main threat of making decision about carrying on business is uncertainty. If it's your first experience of independent activity, then you have no knowledge, no trading skills, no clue about financial organization – not even mentioning the skills of delegation and personnel management.

It results in a situation, when all of the necessary skills and knowledge are being achieved during the process of running a business. Specialist, which is starting up his first business, should keep it in mind.

Ask yourself: which skills are already at your disposal and which are not?

Remember: employment will never provide you the level of revenue you can get by running your own business. If you work for someone, keep in mind that you're being underpaid! It follows from the company's mechanism of earning money.

The second aspect of the same problem is that people come into business because they're getting sick and tired of working under a management of someone else. Any submission means a certain level of the freedom restriction. Sometimes it even means humiliation of dignity, insults or negative attitude. In many cases, the low level of responsibility can also be a cause.

Usually people, who occupy the top positions, used to be a specialists, just like yourself. This means, that people with no appropriate management skills are leading the majority of firms.

Yes, those businesses survive thanks to the energy and enthusiasm of their chiefs, but we cannot talk about any kind of debugged working system in here.

Do you want to succeed? Then create a business, which in its work will be fully independent from you! However, if the main working force in it is you, such business is doomed to fail.

It is quite important to remember, that the problem of incompetent management is very urgent nowadays, especially for the hired specialists who wish to start up their own business. You can thoroughly learn all the aspects of your work but it won't save from such problems as:
1. High stuff turnover rates. You are not able to keep your employee from quitting – you just don't have enough personnel management skills.
2. Shortfall of profit. You just don't know how to maximize its volumes.
3. Lack of the legal remedy. You'll have to puzzle out the ways of registration of your business by yourself.

4. Low organization level and self-motivation. To be a businessman means working very productively and to be well organized: you have to learn how to do that.
5. Low level of discipline in the office.

Problem № 2. Lack of money

The next problem, which causes people to come into business – basic lack of money for personal needs. This category of necessities include:

1. Dating a girl or going to the movies.
2. Spending time with your friends or travelling.
3. Buying new clothes, positive emotions or impressions.
4. Basic necessities and luxury items, etc.

In other words, having money troubles with achieving some goal or making your ideas come to life will push you to the thought of building up your own business in order to create a source or additional income.

Therefore, starting up your own business just to get more money in the first place, you will adapt it to your lifestyle. Business with this sort of philosophy will be aiming for giving its owner not only additional money, but also a freedom.

But what kinds of pitfalls can be hiding in this type of organizing your business?

You should be prepared for getting tired of the field you have chosen pretty quickly – you will start looking for the new ways of increasing your income, try out something new. Partially it happens because you're now looking for the business you would really like to run, you're just looking for more coins.

This approach has both positive and negative sides. But the fact is: that's the main reason dozens of young entrepreneurs came into the world of business – former students, pursuing the idea of fast additional income.

Problem № 3. Responsibility

Our life demands taking more responsibility, as we grow older – for relatives, our colleagues, friends and ourselves. In time, hired working starts to understand that he can improve not only his own standard of living, but his surroundings too.

To be the boss of your life, to take full responsibility for your decisions, help your family, parents and friends – that is the kind of motivation that won't let you stop: you will put all the effort to expanding your business, every resource at your disposal.

Problem № 4. Creating the first source of income

All of us are planning our lives and understand – in the closest (or more long-term) outlook we'll need more money. There can be different reasons for that: addition to the family, moving to another living place, expending your investments, etc. But, sooner or later, you will come to understanding that one day working as an employee won't be able to fulfill your growing needs.

We're all in the search of stability. And that's the one factor you should keep in mind while looking for a job. However, social guarantees you get, working on an employment, has nothing to do with stability itself. Low pension, firing depends on the mood of your chief, salary's not covering up all of your needs – especially if we're talking about planning.

The answer to this problem is building up your own business, which will provide you money now and guarantee your family wealth in the future.

That is the good example of a strategic approach. Such people are ready for long and steady development of their business – so called "long shoulder".

Their business will be similar to steamroller – moving ahead will be slow but steady, with no unnecessary risky moves or fast-taking decisions. You can compare them to farmers as well – they're planting the seeds to harvest much more in a year.

Although, that's not a win-only approach – the problem hides in that the business that can be quickly created is far more effective and easy, than the long-term one. Today it is the fastest the richest.

Speed is an inherent successful business owners' attribute. Otherwise, your rivals will outrun you – those people, who're reading this book right now but are already moving ahead!

Problem № 5. Your boss is a piece of shit

You've got so sick and tired of your boss, that the decision to resign and have your revenge was not long in coming. Moreover, usually these tensions are growing with help of your partner, friend or mentor.

Looking at the business you're working in tells you, that there are tons of more effective management decisions to take. You have a confidence that becoming the owner of your own business would let solve more problems and make your business more profitable.

I have an advice for you: if you feel that way, chop this feeling off at the roots. Otherwise, your hatred of managers, wealth and delegation will strongly affect the success of your own business. Your decisions will work only in the personal aims - often contrary to vitally important interests of company.

Often people leaving on this cause take away with themselves a client base, products and development ideas and begin to work on an analogical chart. Unfortunately, they don't have an understanding, that starting up business from scratch and building it up to the first thousand dollars is pretty easy, but destroying the relationship with the former employer is much worse. It is much more effective to build your future together.

You should also be prepared for being the same chief in the future, so you want to secure your client base, resources, mental, labor and financial capitals from stealing. It can only be provided by automation and complete defense of business, which we will talk about later.

Problem № 6. There's no business teaching at the university

Regularly beginning entrepreneurs start up their own business as the training camp for gaining experience, attempts and mistakes.

I've read an article once and there was a brilliant saying: "There are always two coins they pay you in business – money and experience. Take experience and money won't hesitate."

That saying had a huge influence on me, but now I've come to a conclusion, that you don't need some initial experience for setting up a profitable business. It is possible to combine those two processes, if competently approach to creating and running your own business.

In this book I'll try to explain as detailed as I can about how to start earning money without spending too much time on earning necessary experience. You will learn to combine these two processes: perform these tasks - and get the result!

Problem № 7. "Test it out"/ "Having your own business is in fashion"

There are also categories of people, guided by such kinds of reasons. They come into business because "it's trendy", "my friend had been to a business training", "want to try it out", etc.

I can only hope that you're not one of those people, because otherwise building up a business is not what you're looking for.

If you "want to try", you WON'T REACH the $1000/monthly point.

If you want "to check out" the methods – it WON'T WORK.

In this book, I tell about a systematical approach rather than one-time principles of business organization. The longer you have your own business, the more money it brings – but only if the WORK ON IT.

That is why goals, like "out of interest/check it out/try yourself in it" are doomed to fail.

What should you be prepared for?

Every beginning entrepreneur on his way to success is destined to face the problems, which are pointed out below. To avoid them on your way is like witness a miracle.

These problems are the reasons why 95% of companies perish on their first year of existence. Accept these factors as given and continue to work without paying attention to the obstacles!

1. Relatives

The first thing you'll face with while starting up a business is a distrust and ridicule from your surroundings. "It won't work", "nobody does this", "it's impossible in our country"... The most annoying thing is that the criticism you'll hear will come from the family, the closest people - those who should've strongly supported you.

Of course, the pressure from your surroundings and family is being highly demotivating for anybody – that's why it is so important not to pay too much attention and take a step forward from this stage. It will be all gone the second you will get you first income.

Statistically, only every 4th or 5th business is being successful. It takes a lot of perseverance to make those five attempts, but those people who did it are skimming of the cream.

In my experience, I hear the "prophesies" of that kind from my surrounding every time I start a new project. I stop interacting with those people the moment I hear that, deleting them from my life, which I recommend everyone to do. You don't need negative people in your life! Turn a deaf ear and walk YOUR OWN way!

Only finishing the long way and getting the outcome will make significant changes in your life, including meeting new friends.

2. Absolute impropriety of knowledge

As I've mentioned earlier, the knowledge you get at any government university or college is completely inefficient in the real life.

Usually the skills and knowledge you have after graduating from the university is a useless burden, especially if your business has nothing to do with your specialty.

This happens because the government education system was made to produce, as I call them, "droid-specialists".

If you graduated from any university in Russia or the CIS, then you have no knowledge or experience of organizing and managing your own business.

At the same time, 90% of graduates have these abilities:

- To sit back;
- Lie to the tutors and lecturers;
- Drink alcohol at any amount and at any time;
- Find money for the goals above;
- Search for "gaps" in education system to get the diploma / exam / test for free.

Once you realize the need for any serious knowledge, you have to start your learning all over again - to develop practical skills and acquire ability to do what is required of you.

That is why all the tasks, that will be given at the end of each chapter should be carried out rigorously. With their help, you won't just receive theoretical basis – you will acquire skills, which can then be cloned, scaled, and eventually turned into your own profit.

3. Information is evil.

The moment you will start learning by yourself, getting enormous volumes of information from business trainings and books, you will understand that information is EVIL.

Excess of the information will not lead you to success! The more you read and become acquainted with your market niche, the closer you get to "I know this already" point. As a result, your business becomes boring for you.

This happened to me many times. I had a feeling, that I know everything about my project and it's no longer interesting for me. This is called the effect of the information surplus with the lack of active actions. In order to get a decent outcome you have to DO much more than you KNOW.

<u>The knowledge itself won't get you to the profit.</u>

This book will provide you enough knowledge to lunch your business. I'm not talking about "life-long" business, but you will forget about basic necessities, creating your first own business with about $1000 per month income.

4. Doubt – action

The next level EVERY starting entrepreneur faces with while creating his first project is a level of doubts.

The typical doubts of every man, who starts up his own business, are:

- Will the advert work?
- Is my idea a good choice?
- Will my business be successful?
- Is my way of moving being effective?

Etc.

All these fears are OK and you should be prepared for them. Every businessman has his doubts - the only difference is that successful and experienced ones make fast and accurate decisions under any uncertain circumstances.

The only way to know whether a particular trick will work is to test it on your target audience (run the «pre-launch») in conditions that are close to the real- ones. As a result, a doubt either will become reasonable or will disappear by itself.

Throw away all of your thoughts and give full attention to your actions. Business is a math, not guesswork. Before you do anything - count, count and count again!

5. The dips.

Another obstacle you'll face on your way to creating your own business are so called "dips" (according to the Seth Godin terminology). What are they?

You start your project, get some results and continue developing your business. Although after some time the progress slows down, you start losing money and a recession arises - in other words, the business gets into the dip. Such fluctuations are totally normal, you should just learn to outlive them.

Think of this, are you yourself ready to outlive those dips? Can you overcome all obstacles on your way and become "number one" or, at least, to be among the industry leaders to get a decent profit?

If the answer is "yes" – be prepared. There won't just one or two of those dips on your way. Falling into those and attempts to get out is an infinite process, which will follow your business all the time.

Everything you've read in this chapter is just basic problems that my own or my students' businesses have faced. For each one of the readers the pitfalls will be the same, but doubts, concerns and expectations each has its own.

I'm sure, if you pass the initial level, which usually results in so many quitting entrepreneurs, you get the positive outcome.

Get yourself in tune with a positive mood, move on ignoring all the problems and stop-factors that will be encountered on the way!

Now we move on to the next chapter, of which you'll learn how to set goals that truly work!

Conclusions:

- You do not have to worry about anything. All the obstacles in your way are garbage.

- Doubts are the normal thing. The main point is not to meet them with fear.

- Only a small amount of people is investing in self-education. If you're one of them – congratulations, you're a cut above the gray mass and have everything it takes to become a successful businessman.

Tasks:

1. Figure out the thing that drives you. What makes you think about going into the business?

2. Right down the things, which motivate you. That's a very powerful tool for realizing your wishes and abilities.
3. Remind them yourself each morning.

Chapter 2. Goals. How to choose a business that will survive in the future?

> "At first, I'd imagined how my company should look like, and then just made it happen"
>
> The CEO of IBM

Introduction to the goals

Before you start any doing anything, especially starting your own business, you need to put a specific target, a certain mark, to understand where you want to come.

Talking about the goal setting, I want to show you data from one very interesting research - the so-called "Harvard-Yale experiment". The students of these two legendary universities were asked: "Who of you set goals for life and future?"

The obtained numbers were quite interesting: only 3% of the students had specific goals and plans; 13% kept their goals in mind, not fixing them anywhere; the remaining 84% did not have any goals at all, except as – quote – "to hold out until the summer and pass their exams."

Ten years later, those (now former) students were interviewed once again. It appeared that those 13% "target held in the head" students' average earnings were 2 times higher than those 84%, who had no goals at all.

However, the most surprising thing was that those 3%, who set their goals by writing them down, now earn an average of 10 times (!!!) more than all the others 97% together!

What conclusions can be made out of this data? If you know your goal, it will always be easier to focus on achieving it, as well as give up the distractions in your way.

Those who set their goals, always use those who mindlessly walk along the road of life. If you do not work for your dream and desires in the current unit of time, then you work for other people to reach their goals.

It's not always obvious, like in the case of employment, but to some extent this principle is most often used in the following:

- Programs embedded in us by our parents, to help you realize their unrevealed purpose, inherit their complexes and so on;
- In the tasks and goals of other business owners;
- In the tasks and goals of your friends and family;
- In your teacher's installations, who took over the part of your education, etc.

> \- Where should I swim, Master? Downstream or upstream?
>
> \- Swim wherever you need to be.

Once you put yourself a landmark of where you want to get, everything will be much easier and more obvious. In this chapter, we shall now define your goals and discover how exactly you will understand that you've reached them.

Questions before we start.

Before starting up a business, we should agree on what it means. Business is a tool, a mechanism, which helps you to reach what you want.

In order to launch this mechanism you have to understand: why do you even need your own business? What goal is that you're chasing? To earn money? If yes, then how much? If your goal is filling yourself with emotions, then you have to discover which emotions you are looking for, etc.

In addition, you need to answer a series of questions that will help you with finding your market niche and a way of creating your own business:

• How much money do you need for a comfortable existence in life? (Stabilization Fund / Minimum / Comfort / Chick / Wealth);

• How much money do you want to get from your business?

• How much free time per day / week / month / year you want to have, owning your own business?

• What lifestyle do you want to keep using your own business?

• What do you want to achieve in business?

• What will you perfect day look like? (When will you wake up, go to bed, how will you spend your day, with whom, etc.)

• How do you imagine your business-day? (Where do you work – home/web/office, how much time per week, with whom, etc.)

• When will you understand that your business is successful?

• What are you not ready to do at all? (Paint the walls / distribute flyers / communicate with people / sell, etc. - all of these responsibilities should be delegated to someone)

• How won't you spend your time in the business for sure? (For example, "I will not sit in an office all day")

• How will you understand that you need to quit this business? (For example, when your idea didn't work)

As for me, I often use a technique I've leant when I was engaged in securities trading. Traders set either a goal to be achieved («Take Profit»), or exit-point to stop the transactions, when the losses are already becoming serious («Stop-Loss»).

You must also set conditions, under which you will leave your business if it suffers losses. Keep in mind that you should quit only at the moment of reaching the set target. Learn to turn off your emotions and plan your actions in advance!

The sequence of events law.

<u>If the business is being followed by the same problem, this will continue until any drastic changes are made. And there are no reasons for changing of this course of events.</u>

Consequence of Murphy's Law

- Who surrounds you? Who are these men?

- What experience do you already have:

  - sales;
  - creating systems ;
  - organization of events;
  - delegation and working with co-workers?

- For how long are you creating your business – 1 year / 5 years / 10 years / 50 years / 200 years? How long will it exist?

- What are you doing now? How does your job differ from planned business?

- What can stop you? What can prevent you from reaching this goal? Do not neglect your shortcomings – stay opened to your weaknesses, it will help to "close" them!

- What motivates you? For what are you ready to wake up early in the morning? What can help you on the way to the target (define some small "Pleasantness")?

Answer these questions right now. Yes – RIGHT NOW! Yes, take a piece of paper, a pen and WRITE DOWN the answers! I'm being serious – now, right when you're reading these lines. I'll wait.

I'm still waiting! Come on, right it down for God's sake!

Excellent. Move on as you finish.

Financial calculation.

Now we will calculate how to get the income you want to achieve, and at the same time define the cost of an hour of your work.

Similarly to the weightlifting, in order to get the desired income you have to take the weight, which you are able to "lift" – it's an occasion to recheck your goal right now and possibly swap to more achievable.

So you've putted the really attainable goal for yourself – $1000 per month. How can you get this money?

Option № 1. $1000 is one wholesale deal.

If you're profit is 5% per deal, you need to strike only one $20 000 bargain per month.

Software, products of "b2b" segment and supply retail can be used as a commodity.

Option № 2. Your plan is 1000 items with a $1 profit each.

This volume is easy to reach by creating a web-store, a kiosk, a retail, etc. If you have a 50% profit, you need 2000 mass consumption goods, which will be bought quickly. This requires only a stream of buyers.

Option № 3. You need just ten units with $100 profit. If a product makes you $100 (a profit expected if selling mobile phones, electronics, lighting systems, etc.), then 10 transactions per month only will achieve the planned amount.

Having defined the needs and way of doing business, throw out the ones you're not interested in, and highlight the segment in which you want to work.

<u>Business is a math. The key to success - the replication of the same things regularly and thoughtfully. Counting in business prevails over creativity.</u>

1. Let's talk about the cost of one hour of your work. We will need it to keep a track of:

a) your efficiency;

b) how much money can be spend on hiring people;

c) how much do you "cost" as a manager at the moment.

We count this number as follows:

1. Add all the profits for the last 3 months, for example:

$450 + $600 + $550 = $1600

2. Then divide the sum by the number of hours of each month (there's about 170 working hours per month).

1600 / (3 * 170) = $ 3.1 / hour

Calculating this figure, you also know how much you can pay to an employee for an hour to take off the chore.

2. Then we need to calculate how much money is required to launch your business idea – simply speaking, to determine your costs.

I want to specify – if you follow the plan as described in this book, and perform all the tasks, you don't need to spend more than $ 200-300 to start up your businesses. Yes, nothing is free!

Count down how much money is there in your pocket and how much you'll be able to borrow from your friends, buddies or relatives.

The essence of calculations is not only in taking into the account the potential profit and in visualizing it. You should also calculate the money, which will be invested in the business, as well as measure the possible financial losses you might have.

Motivation.

Beside the fact, that you will be criticized by people and the problems I've mentioned earlier will try to be an obstacle for you, there will be something good – "light at the end of tunnel", as I call it. That light is where you're going to.

You've already answered the question about how you see your future life. However, that's not over - give the answers to the following:

- What do you want to have?

- Where you want to go?

- What do you want to be able to do?

- What do you want to experience?

- What motivates you?

You need to write down your answers, because in the business world only personal desires, only the things you really want will help you to wake up in the morning, go crazy about your idea and do your work with joy and enthusiasm!

If you want a car, apartment or a house – that's just PERFECT! Write it down, print their pictures and hang them on the visualization board. Make your own Dream Board!

Put some little reminders about your desires all over the places. You should always keep in mind the answer to the question – "WHY DO I EVEN DO THIS? WHERE DO I GO? "

If you want a family, emotions, skills, situations – just express it on paper. Make a list of goals you're aiming for!

I have this list hanging with attached photos on the board behind me, so that I could always turn around and see what is behind all my actions!

<u>If you do not reward yourself, why do you even do this?</u>

Along your path, you will rarely hear the kind words, especially in the beginning. My advice is to note them using video, audio, text, post them in your blog - let you be your personal "success journal".

Note all the nice words you hear during the day in it, and all the things that you've "finalized" (reached logically complete results). Personally, I like to keep my "Live Journal" or online-diary so other people can be aware of my achievements.

In the darkest days, you'll be able to open your "success journal", read it and get rid of doubts and discouragements, to continue its work with renewed enthusiasm.

When to quit the business?

> "The most important condition for success is a self-discipline.
>
> Either you work on yourself or you degrade"
>
> - Mikhail Khodorkovsky

Another important aspect, which I will touch on right now, can be stated as – "when you have to quit your business?"

Be prepared for the fact that not all of your projects will be successful. The purpose of this book is to give you an algorithm with which you'll be able not only to create one or even several businesses, but also to repeat your success and scale it in the unlimited quantities.

Why do we need to set criteria, which indicate that this particular project is a failure?

The answer is very simple – we do this so you won't give up too soon. I always recommend writing down the criteria that would mean that the project failed. For example: "the debt has exceeded..." "we're not getting any profit since ..." etc.

You have to understand that business should bring you profit IMMEDIATELY and demand for your first offer should be present initially. Thanks to the techniques described in this book, you will obtain profits from your businesses INSTANTLY, rather than wait for a miracle.

In order to smash through the board with your fist you have to aim behind it. To set the right goals and the right "STOPs", aim behind them!

Closing the "STOP" you'll carry some losses NOW, but will find yourself strategically winning, working through your discipline and saving resources to start the next project.

Seven steps to setting business goals.

> "Wellbeing everywhere depends on two conditions: setting the correct ultimate goals and finding appropriate means, leading to them"
>
> - Aristotle

There are seven steps to describe a goal of your business properly and each of one of them is some orientation point with which you should always check.

This technology helps you to tune in to the task and orient your subconscious properly to move to your goal as one piece. Take a pen, a sheet of paper and go through this chapter, describing each step.

Step 1 - setting an obvious result.

This is what we have already talked about - the result can be a financial indicator, as well as some kind of a lifestyle you desire, or some other enjoyable things. In other words, your goal should be determined by an obvious result - you have to understand exactly what you want to get.

There are 2 types of goals:

Positive. "I want a car, freedom, travel, etc." This is the motivation "to something" - a place, situation or experience where you want to get.

Negative. "I want to avoid, I want to remove, to get away from, etc." This is the motivation "away from something" when you have a desire to get away, get rid of something, take away the pain of your life.

For our goals, we will use only positive type of goal setting. Business cannot assist something you want to avoid - it needs its own positive goal!

Step 2 - setting your area of responsibility or answer to the question "what exactly are you doing in business?"

Answer this question not in the future tense (I will only deal with bookkeeping or just hiring staff), but in the present one, as if your own business is already running.

Write a valuable final product of your business (VFP). What amount of VFP will your business produce?

Step 3 - defining the environment.

Who do you want to develop your business with? Who will be with you to work towards achieving your goals?

You should imagine whether you create a business "for yourself", "for a client" or business with management departments. Will you yourself solve all the problems or you will have partners from the very beginning? How many? Who will set the strategic and tactical goals?

In accordance with the concept of this book, I recommend creating a business you, completely taking full responsibility and hiring staff for routine tasks only.

Step 4 - setting time limits.

You need to answer the question: "How quickly can you build your business?" Set a realistic time frame. Businessman has to understand whether he's moving in the right direction and at the speed, which was originally expected.

There's an obvious difference between achieving revenue of $ 1,000 per month in two years or in a week. Both are real, but the speeds of achieving this goal are different.

Write down a specific date when you plan to reach the required level of income, but do not fool yourself because otherwise the effect will be reversed.

This book can be used for 1 month working at a "full involvement" rate, for 2 months of moderate rate or for 3 months to work at the "easy" pace.

Step 5 - setting restrictions.

You need to put the "STOPs" for a well-timed exit from business to prevent the growth of losses. We've talked about it earlier.

Step 6 - subconscious verification.

This step is a self-test: how interested are you in doing one business or another? If at this point you feel that the chosen niche doesn't suit you, you should change it. In the same way you need to break up with your partners if there is a suspicion that they might fool you.

At this stage you need to answer the following questions:

- How will customers react to your business?

- Will this project be a "one-time" thing to make a quick profit, or do you prefer to organize the "life-long" business?

Just sit down, relax, close your eyes for a few minutes and imagine your future projects. Adjust everything written, focusing on the final result.

Step 7 - defining the available resources.

This step answers the question: "What vital resources are currently at your disposal?"

- money
- time
- knowledge
- skills

- connections

What is their volume you are ready to invest in your business to get the result (hours per day, the amount of money, connections you use, etc.)?

Make your first step today!

Start doing simple, clear things that will start moving you to your destination. Take responsibility for the business yourself – I assure you, it's worth it.

Lifestyle

I want to pay a special attention to your lifestyle and your business –what way do you live.

During my life I've organized a lot of businesses, being an owner of companies, developing which made me live in the office, as well as the firms, managing which I've traveled around the globe, doing things remotely.

You have to discover the way you want to live and the business will be the tool for achieving those desires.

Create a business that will make your desired lifestyle come true. Every dream can come to life, whether those are VIP-parties or just peaceful family life. For each of those there are different areas and ways of doing business: choose the method that suits you. This is how you maximize your results!

Preparing for the business creation – drawing a portrait of your surroundings.

Doing this stage is recommended, but it's not being obligatory. If you're not seeing the necessity in it then just skip to the next chapter.

The next step in making groundwork for starting your own business is drawing a kind of a portrait of your surroundings. Describe those people you would like to work with.

Perhaps you prefer working with women, business owners or cooperating with a particular group of people.

Keep in mind that that's not your target audience, but just some general characteristics of people you feel COMFORTABLE to work with. People that you prefer to interact with creating some values. These are your needs and a business will be a mechanism of satisfying them.

The same way you should describe the people you don't want to work with – clients, partners and workers you wish you wouldn't see beside yourself. It should be done before you choose you niche – set your own rules and conditions. For example:

- "I'm not working with stupid people and criteria of stupidity is my own personal opinion";

- "We're successful because we work with…"
- "We have good results because we don't work with…"

Now let's turn to the making of the list of you skills.

Write sown all of the skills and knowledge you have ever used in your life, including the oddest ones. For example:

- Delegating the changing of light bulbs to a neighbor;
- Ability to give tasks to the freelancers;
- Ability to "push" people into keeping their promises;
- I have a skill of managing private freelancers;
- I have a skill of negotiating with elder women, etc.

All the information we get will help us a little bit later.

You should know what you can do by yourself and what you should delegate to the others. To make it possible write down all the basic skills and fundamental knowledge you have. Recall all of your useful connections – those necessary people you have in your phonebook.

Conclusions:

• Set clear goals of your business development!

• Answer the question – why do you need your business?

• Calculate not only your potential profits, but also possible losses.

• Once in a while, calculate those key indicators - the cost of your work per hour and the business opening expenditures.

• Motivate yourself!

• Business should allow you to have a lifestyle you want.

• Surround yourself with people you feel comfortable to work and communicate with.

Tasks:

1. Spent 5 minutes writing as many nice things, useful skills and positive emotions you want to experience, as you expect to get during your life.

2. Make your visualization board.

3. Create your own blog and post your successes there.

4. Write down a goal of your business, comparing it with the seven steps described above.

5. Conceptualize your lifestyle.

6. Draw a portrait of your surroundings.

Chapter 3. Juridical Issues

Many people launching their first business are asking themselves: "What would happen if..."

- "Revenue service comes"

- "Customers will buy, and I won't be able to..."

- "Working capital exceeds one million..."

- "Should I register as a SP or LLC?" Etc.

In this chapter we will talk about the legal issues "practice" of doing business – how they are solved in the real life.

Revenue service

When you create your first business, and we are talking about the income of $1000-5000 per month, the revenue service just doesn't care.

There's no need to register your business as a legal entity right from the start unless you're working in the «B2B» segment or you offer any intermediary services (under the agency agreement).

It is also necessary if you operate with large sums liable to VAT from the beginning – then having registration as a legal entity will be extremely important for your work.

<u>A legal entity status is a symbol of trust in the relationship inside the market. It affects the conversion and ways you receive payments for your goods or services, as well as gives you the opportunity to work with the biggest customers. In everything else, it's a secondary factor.</u>

What do I choose – SP or LLC?

As for me, the best solution was to register as a sole proprietorship (SP) to pay a small amount of taxes each quarter, which is much easier. You can be registered very quickly – in 2 or 3 days.

Customers don't care whether you're an SP or LLC – it doesn't affect their trust. If they buy the product, then it doesn't depend on the form of ownership.

The registration of LLC makes sense only if you start a business with partners. The difference with SP is that in the event of bankruptcy, LLC is liable to the creditors with not a personal but only with corporate property. However, nobody will give you credits for the first few years, so there's no need to complicate your life.

What to do with inspections?

Fear of inspections is a normal reaction. It is important to understand that when you first start a business with small working capital nobody shall come to you with a tax inspection because any serious test would simply kill your project.

Register SP and you will submit reports at the end of the quarter: it allows you to "finalize" your reporting to the desired form. Wait in line to register, pay a fee, find out all the conditions yourself – it takes a little time but invaluable experience you receive would come in handy. That's why you shouldn't delegate the registration of SP to anyone else – do it all yourself.

"Shakedown" and "protection"

I encountered a shakedown by the state (or rather a local deputy) only once. Now I realize that all of this could have been avoided – the lawyers explained how it was possible to get rid of such things. Everything comes with experience!

While your business is at the very start, nobody needs it. There's just nothing to "take away". Another thing if you have an existing revenue stream: creating it, you should start to implement security systems.

How to close the deal without being a legal entity?

If you went down the "profit first, then entity" road and faced with the need to close the deal through a checking account, then:

1. Pay attention to your surroundings.

Most likely, some of your friends probably have a contact with a person who is an individual entrepreneur or have a registration as a legal entity. You can always ask them to receive a transfer from your customers on their checking account.

As for me, I have received the transfers with the help of friends many times – usually customers just don't care who owns the company.

2. Agency contract.

If you need to make a transaction and get paid for it, then connect people through this kind of a contract. The status of SP, LLC or other forms of property is not required to do this.

You can easily download its template online. Each transaction is a separate contract with your prescribed fee.

3. If you have any questions and you need the answers, then there is a great technique: I call it the "AYL"-technique – "Ask your lawyer!""

Find a man who knows these matters, a friend who has some connections or just call in the law agency – all the details will be told and all aspects of needed operations will be clarified. It's ok not to know everything: the main point – just find out all the information you need.

Get used to communicate with experts in various fields and talk to the experts who understand your problem, especially when it comes to advice on legal issues.

Conclusions:

- Don't worry – at the start, tax audits are harmless to your business.
- SP is the best form of registration for the beginning entrepreneur.
- Do the registration yourself and gain the experience that you may need.
- If you do not want to bother with registration at first, then just make a deal through your friends firms.
- Find out where you can get qualified legal consultation!

Tasks:

1. Find a lawyer friend or law agency, which employees' competence can be trusted.

Chapter 4. What is business? Defining some terms before the start.

What is business?

In order that we can fully understand each other, let's specify some aspects. We must operate with the same concepts and right now, we shall clarify the meaning of certain categories.

1. What does the word "business" mean to you?

For some it's earning money, providing services or sales. However, for me it is, primarily, SATISFYING HUMAN NEEDS.

So, the business is satisfying needs of people by providing services or goods of a certain value. Notice that vector of your activities must be directed outside. You give, you present, you provide value and you give what people need.

<u>You are not your client. You have to sell what is needed by people, not by you.</u>

2. Satisfying the needs of the client.

Satisfaction means that you're doing more than people expect or at least, do something proportionate to their expectations. You're satisfying human needs, otherwise customers will not come back for the next purchase.

Discrepancy to this rule causes functioning of aging business models. For example, a one-time purchase model, when entrepreneur does not think about long-term relationship with the client, trying to "withdraw" the maximum amount of cash for just one time.

I faced this in China, when I wanted to buy jeans. Because I didn't know their average price, I bought jeans for a price, that was 4 times higher than real – a good example of the business aimed at single purchases.

I've never come back, not only to that store, but to that place at all. At that time, the shop owner won due to my ignorance, but in the long run he lost. I've left with unmet need, which means I "closed" it by purchasing good, but didn't satisfy.

3. Value.

Value is a quality of goods or services, which is important for the client in a problem of meeting his needs. Value is what attracts a person and a reason he wants to buy the product or use the service.

However, there is a difference between what the customer wants and what he really needs. Often, selling goods, are you sure that man NEEDS this product to close the need, reduce expenditures, increase sales, etc. Though, he won't buy it because he doesn't WANT it. He wants something else, some benefits, for example.

You need to sell what people want and provide what they need. For example, you can sell beauty, health and sexy body, and provide a course of sport-dance lessons.

Types of business

Earlier, I mentioned some of the terms that you will see below. Now we will discuss them one by one.

«B2C» - «Business to client». The selling of goods, services, solutions for the end user, the person who will use the product directly. If you've opened a barbershop then it's a business «B2C». Same thing if you sell retail clothing to the person who will wear it. In the «B2C» business type you work with the end customers.

«B2B» - «Business to Business». In this type, you work to provide services, products and solutions to other business.

"B2B" has just a few niches:

- Increasing sales;

- Increasing productivity;

- Cost reduction;

- Improving the quality of the system itself;

- Automation of the system;

- Creating a new source / center of profit.

All of B2B-sector companies operate in these niches one way or another. For example, if you sell rice boilers for restaurants, it increases productivity and helps them to automate the work of your clients' personnel.

The higher level of business contacts, high working capital and more interesting (for me, for example) bargains are typical for B2B business.

"Being pushy".

Another component of the business is a way you get to know about the deal. For example, you can first buy an item, and then start tries to sell it. In this case, you don't know the audience, which needs it, don't know the value of this good – in other words, you try to "push" it to anyone at a profitable price.

I've seen it many times: friends of mine decided to start selling caviar – first they have found a product, and then decided to sell it. Of course, they didn't bother with the answers to the questions: "to whom to sell?" and "how to sell?"

Selling. First, you find people and identify their need, and then you satisfy it. In order to do this, you should:

- Make a deal, take an advance payment for a solution to their problems;

- Solve the problem and close the deal;

- Acquired money you invest in attracting new customers.

Afterwards, this chain repeats itself and this is the biggest difference between this method of selling goods or services and the previous one.

Previous method is more risky and difficult. Because you are the one, who's interested in selling an item you've purchased. You suffer from the costs of the warehouse where the remaining goods are being stored, depreciation, and loss in the price of goods.

In the second case, you're making a deal at a time when customers are already found, so there is no fear that you won't be able to sell the goods. A good example is a drop shipping (custom trade).

Need – the main enemy of the closed deal

"Odessa-style business". 5 easy ways for partisans to quickly create a business "from scratch".

During my practice, I found five easy ways to quickly build up your business "from scratch", which immediately begins to make a profit.

Each of these methods has its own advantages and disadvantages. I've tried all of them, that's why you can be sure that they were tested in the real life. The basic concept of these paths is a quick start with minimal risk.

WARNING! These pathways **differ from the classical way of organizing your own business**, which I describe in the main part of the book. So, if you feel that you've captured the essence, then you can start up already in this chapter!

Method 1. "To leech" – "sit down" on someone else's stream of customers with your product or service.

The basic concept of this approach is that you need to find a business that works successfully already. This future "donor" must meet the following conditions:

- profitable;
- has a large incoming stream of customers;
- has it's own client database;
- not able to monetize it – optional.

For example, let's take a barbershop. About 100 people come here every day – they get a haircut and pay for it.

Your task is to find such a place and start providing similar services that are not competitive, comparing to the CURRENT business,

You find a "donor" like that, negotiate with him, and place your own business in his area. For example, when it comes to the barbershop, it can be a manicurist, working on their customer stream. This way you start earning money from the very first day you!

Of course, you will be asked to pay the interest for this. This is quite reasonable, and you will have to give away a certain amount of income.

Not only offline businesses, such as:

- Barber ("point" - manicurist);

- Shoe store ("point" - Salon shoe repair);

- Accessories ("point" - Audio CDs);

- Etc.,

Can be "donors", but also companies working online. In this case you put your product on the showcase of another online store. Almost everyone does it – I don't know about you, but I've never met online retailers who own items or keep them in storage themselves.

Get it? Then do it!

Method 2. "Leaning" to a big client.

In this method, you will only need one big client. Then you find the need he wants to be satisfied. For example, we begin to supply a company that sells air conditioners, with spare parts or accessories in a huge volume.

The basic concept of this method is meeting the need in any product or service for a big client. For example, to develop an application for Skype, start providing the sushi restaurants network with packages, etc.

You get the first order right away and so it is already possible for to build up a company, and then find other small, medium and large customers and make deals with them.

How exactly can you start working this way?

- Search through friends and co-workers, and meet with the owner of this kind of company.

- Offer him more favorable conditions, bypassing secretaries and purchasing agents. A key aspect is not just providing goods from outside, but creating your company within the structure of his firm.

At the same time you get one very important advantage – you can use the name and resources of their company for your own purposes. This technique can be compared to the creation of autonomy within the country.

- Once you find the second big customer, begin to position yourself as a separate company.

2. Entering business as a consultant.

"Consultant is the man who takes your watch and then tells you what time it is"

This method assumes that you come into the business and start working on improving it – not as a full-time employee, but as an independent expert.

Advantage of this approach is that you won't be the one who takes damage because of the errors you make – it will be a firm that uses the your services.

Successful solutions will show what works in this business, and what doesn't and the financial returns from successful solutions shall cover your concerns with a vengeance. Normal price of the consultation for small businesses will be $1000 monthly + bonus – an interest received from the company profits.

There are some difficulties in such entering, but they are manageable if desired. "Step by step"-scheme will look like this:

- choose the niche;
- "enter" 3-4 businesses as a consultant;
- select all the methods and techniques that really work in this niche;
- create your own similar business after a while (7 months - year).

During this time, you will earn enough money to supply yourself with enough amount of money, as well as to develop your business to acceptable level of profitability.

How to become a consultant? Just google it. There is enough material on this topic.

When searching for the first customers to consult, pay attention to the "cold" calls, "cold" tour, searching clients via friends and direct marketing. If there are more questions - Google knows everything!

3. Cloning an existing business

I developed this approach after visiting famous business training. Its essence is to become partners with foreign businessmen, and then get their business to the market of your country!

Basically, you take those niches that are already successful, meaning they've made good money for their owners. Call, get in touch and transfer his store, advertising or hosting to your market.

This technique would be perfect for online stores and retail: you're just transferring resources and advertising campaign, and then just make a profit. In case of the online store, the hosting site (see "hosting" – google.com) can leave the custody of the new partner, but domain must be registered on you.

I used this method when I was launching the web-store of the erotic costumes: I transferred it to Ukraine from Russia with a help of magnificent businessman Annie. Her website is ero-costume.ru – check it out.

Use a little ingenuity and you will see how this scheme can tolerate the maximum benefit of retail outlets. It is always difficult to sell the first business as a franchise, but if it was efficient, then other attempts will be successful.

4. Solutions for the target audience or how to earn your first money right away

Solution that you provide depends on the target audience for which it was designed. What does it give?

You have a base – you already know with whom to communicate among your surroundings. You can find out what is required for this audience and start a business from that. In other words, you begin to deliver your surroundings what they need and then just scale this business to an "external" market.

You can call your friends right now, have a little chat and discover what do they need, what problems do they have, and which one you can solve.

At first, you do that for one person, then for the second, the third ... view the general trend – if there is a similar problem for 100-200 people, how can you solve it? In this case, you do not have to provide a product or service yourself, you can start from a position of mediator.

So, begin to solve this issue, close your problem. The first client, the second – and you already have your unique business, tied up to a specific value of your product or service.

In searching for a solution for a specific TA start from the requirements of client database. You can deliver hookahs and fashionable clothes to students in your surroundings, and provide consulting services, automation and raw materials to the businessmen at the same time. In this case, you ARE NOT TIED UP to the product!

Scheme of doing things will look like this:

1. Phone your friends and acquaintances;

2. Communicate and find the problem to be solved;

3. Ask: "would it be interesting for you to solve this issue (buy this product, get a service, etc.)?"

4. Waiting – if you get the answer "yes", then

5. Take 2-3 days' timeout to find a solution;

6. Closing the deal.

This way I sold online-stores, SEO-promotion services, SMM, tools, construction materials, and grain for export. Similarly, I am constantly practicing one-time transaction deals. All that is required from you in this case is to be alert and aware of the needs of the people around you, your colleagues, friends and acquaintances.

You cannot build the full value business on this scheme – it's still a one-time deal, although they appear relatively regularly, based on your contacts. But they will help to always earn money anyway.

You're usually earned about 10-25% of the profits on such transactions, because you're proving only agency services. A profit from sales of this kind depends on the number of your contacts and personal sales skills.

You should practice this type of deals anytime, anywhere – even after you will choose your own business niche.

Read the books:

- "Never Eat Alone" by Kate Ferrazzi;

- Darcy Rezacs' "Work the pond";

- "Everything is negotiable" by Gavin Kennedy.

Draw conclusions, install them into this of contracts and receive profits!

WARNING!

Before the next chapter, read and draw the conclusions!

<u>*Models of building a business.*</u>

There are two models of building a business.

The first model - the so-called "cash cow" – is a business that was built only for making profit. This is a typical model of any medium-sized businesses - the man builds business "from himself" and "for himself".

Standard construction of business - a "cash cow" - involves a lot of problems and nuances. Typically, accounting is being made on occasions - on Saturdays and Sundays, also with not everything clear and transparent with taxes. Over time, there are many debts, people are trying to pull out money - as a loan or as a return of duty, and therefore such companies often have debts.

The second model, which is more practical and productive - business for sale. Business is being built with the expectation that it will be sold later. You immediately know that your job is to "pack it up" in such a way that it would attract the next investor. You know the type of investor, for which you organize the business, and look for the same type of investors to sell them - one business or several businesses one by one.

What is the problem? Man builds a business that brings him money, with the dream that someday he will sell the business. At the same time, he initially organizes business processes thoughtlessly, without thinking about future sales and attracting investors.

If you put a saddle on a cow and try to participate in the race, you shall never be the one who wins. And most likely, you won't come to the finish line at all. The same thing in business – don't do the "cash cow" out of your business, if in the future you plan to participate in a race with horses.

No financial investor will be driven by the idea of buying a "cash cow" business, which has a whole bunch of problems and nuances. Business shouldn't be built so that its creator would be caged inside a revolving wheel with a bunch of people, branches, processes around, running in the wheel like a squirrel.

How to check whether the business was built correctly? Go on a vacation. When a person walks away from his business - a week, two, three, or a month - and sales are down by 30%, that means only one thing: the pyramid was built incorrectly. Accordingly, there are problems with development, because due to the statistics the number of "rays" diverging from the person should not exceed 16, otherwise he's just not physically able to perform his duties. Average number of "rays" shouldn't be more than 5-7.

There are ways to properly build a "cash cow" and also there are ways to build a business for sale.

Even if you see that the business looks like a "cash cow", such a model can be "packed" and "cloned" in the future. There can be different options for "packaging" - the systems of making money on the web studio, studio design, programming, etc.

That means, you can "pack" business model, which visually resembles a "cash cow", but if this "cow" can provide a great income for your target audience, not for you personally, then it can be sold very successfully.

It is clear that for the owner of working business and for a man who only launches one, the concept of the "big income" does not mean the same thing.

(c) Andrew Parabellum

Business plan. Myth or Reality?

> "KiS - Keep it Simple"
>
> Microsoft slogan.

No matter how many businesses I've created, around me always was a man who asked – "do you have a business plan on 45 pages? Without it, nothing happens!"

Often, these "experts" are the proud owners of brilliant ideas, maybe even a few business plans. But they do not have the main thing – currently working business. Just thinking and theory.

In this book I examine the practical side – something that is appropriate to our situation, where we will not take loans and immediately build a multimillion-dollar production concern.

Business plan will look like A4 sheet of paper for you, on which the numbers of expected income / expense, the expected profit and conclusions are written – how quickly the business will pay off and where the first acquired money will go.

If your business plan does not fit on A4 paper, then it doesn't work: rewrite and simplify it.

You have to understand what you're going to do: it should be easy for you. Later you will complicate and build an "alarm systems" in your business – now you should just earn money.

Conclusions:

- Business is satisfying the needs of people.
- The main thing that encourages the client to make the purchase is a value of goods or services.
- There are five easy ways to start up your own profitable business – use them!
- Business consulting is a great way to "get" into the top management of the client.
- Business plan is a calculation, which gives you understanding of how quickly your expenses will pay off. It must not take up more than one sheet of A4.

Tasks:

- Prepare yourself and make the decision to create a specific business;
- Think of a simple business plan using the ways listed above and begin to initiate those partisan starts;
- Meet five millionaires and ask them what they need for their business;

- Close these deals;

- Suggest consultation services to at least 50 companies. You will develop them using either this book or another. Initially, sell it and then decide later, when the money will be on hand, which shall preform that.

- "Look through" the businessmen you know – who need your product or service? Sell it to them.

Chapter 5. Finding the niche

Here we come to the most "delicious" thing in this book – the classical approach to the creation of businesses. We've discussed the definitions, chose the form of incorporation, set yourself some goals, and defined your lifestyle. Now it's time to start up a business.

How to formulate your niche?

Formulating you niche will help you and your customers clearly understand who you are and what do you do. What is "formulated niche"? Generally speaking, it is the answer to the following questions:

- What is on sale?
- Who do you sell to?
- Why is it beneficial?
- What does it have?

An example from my life:

"Business for young people who create their own business and have an income of up to $500 of it."

Let's try to answer the questions above:

- "What?" – Business clothes;
- "Who?" – Young people;
- "Why is it beneficial?" – It is difficult to find a business class clothing with an income of $500;
- "What are the competitive advantages?" Uniquely chosen combination – "business clothing / income up to $500". Every guy wants to be a businessman!

That is exact kind of clothes I've supplied to my customers. Guys, who were starting their own business, came to find a stylish shirt and a jacket, to dress up for appropriate amount of money. By the way, I advise you to pay attention to this niche – it is almost empty now.

Accordingly, in the example there is a clear indication of the target audience, which are guys (I did not sell clothes for the girls).

Formulate your niche by answering those four questions. It's time to practice a little – write down your answers!

- For whom? (for businesses, shops, boys, children, etc.)
- Why is it beneficial for them? Under what conditions? (for those who are looking for quality, moved into a new house, only brown furniture, with a turnover of...)

• Why from you? What are the advantages, benefits? (disposable, speed, quality, price, density, etc.)

Formulate a niche by answering these questions. Write out 15-20 categories of goods or services and reformulate them so that the niche would sound correctly, simply it, and show benefits to the customer.

Portrait of the target audience or "for whom is our niche?"

Once you've formulated your niche, we need to understand the language in which to talk with your target audiences to attract it?

We need to fully explore the audience to get maximum results from advertising.

Let me explain with an example. You can offer just dancing, but you can also offer slimming dancing, stylish dances, crash course "perfect body in three months", "New American program for weight loss", "the perfect model of the club seduction", etc. In fact, all of these are dancing, but depending on the chosen form, they are "knocking" to the different audiences, selling your services to a different people.

The tool, which we're looking at now, will help us to understand is what situation is our potential customer and what the advertising message will push him towards our offer.

In order to do this, take a sheet of A4-paper and draw a similar pattern:

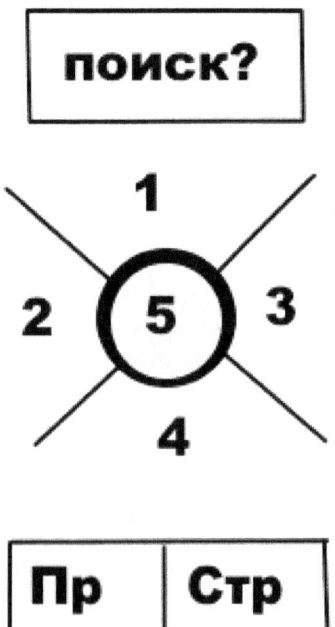

In **the first paragraph** we enter bosses or those people who have an influence on our potential client.

For example, take such goods as an ugg boots. Here we're aiming for girls students. Let's call our representative of the target audience Masha. Masha is a typical student, 24 years old.

She's feeling the pressure of the deanery, parents, and maybe even bosses, if Masha is smart and got herself a job.

And all those sides of the influence constantly tell her:

- "Study better";
- "Attend classes";
- "Be more modest";
- "Stop acting like…" etc.

We write out the category and what our potential costumers specifically hear from this category.

Do you begin to understand how to sell ugg boots through education?

The second paragraph – who are her friends and relatives of the second circle?

Masha has female friends, the same students who want to be different, to look fashionable, sexy and stylish. This means that there is another channel through which we can "reach" Masha.

The third paragraph – on the right, we write down the following information: who are her colleagues at work? Who support or, contrariwise, doesn't support her? Who helps her to make a purchasing decision? Is she dependent on colleagues' opinion? Who influences her?

We're writing all of that, and the more, the better.

4. Below, we indicate whom Masha influences.

She can have her own pupils, she can give private lessons or she might even communicate with less beautiful, not as stylish girls. In other words, we can assume that these are the people, who are listening to her opinion with an open mouth.

Accordingly, we can give her benefits through patronage or the opportunity to become an example for her friends – and in the same way sell our products to her "followers" and "copycats".

5. The circle in the center it's our ideal customer, our Masha. We enter her name, age, annual / monthly / weekly earnings (depending on the product), what is her job, her geographical location, actions, etc. The more precise and specific portrait we make, the stronger our offer will be!

Do not be afraid to make your audience smaller: in any case, the other people will buy your product too. One day my friend, Paul Podobed, was telling me about his adventure – the ducks hunt. The essence of this story was a very good phrase:

"You can shoot the one particular duck, only by aiming at one. You cannot bring it down, firing at random into a flock of birds..."

Think about it.

Then we turn to the lower blocks of our sheet of paper.

On the left side, we specify all the problems our Masha encounters, everything she wants to get rid of her life, what she hates and what makes her angry.

There may be many of those things – stepping on her foot on the subway, jealousy of her friends, rainy weather, failing an exam at the university, etc. Each everyday problem opens us a window into her purse!

On the right side, we specify everything she seeks and dreams about. Everything that makes her wakes up in the morning. For example, finding a job, finding her "prince", cooking soup for the loved one in the kitchen, relaxing in the club on Friday, seeing the envy in the eyes of her friends, etc.

Anyway, we write down all the things she wants and she wants to do, to feel in her life.

The next paragraph is how the man will look for your product.

In what ways and under what conditions there is a need in our product? Will it be an online store or a person will go to the shopping mall? At that moment, what will he feel, think, etc.

Don't be lazy; give this work as much time as you can! If you would just describe like this – manager, 20-27 years old, with earnings of $500-1000, it won't be a clear target audience. How are you going to reach him? What will you say?

If so will formulate like this – a girl, a student, the 3rd year, the city of Omsk – then reaching her with your message becomes much easier. This portrait can even be used in advertising: "You're a girl? Student? 3rd year? Omsk? Excellent – our product is just for you!" – and it will work.

The more precisely you highlight your target audience, the easier it will be to come up with ways to promote your goods or services.

Two simple tools for choosing a niche on the Internet

How to understand the demand of a particular niche? For these there are two very interesting online tools – with their help we can find the demand for goods and services without the extra effort.

These tools are called «Google Adwords» and «Wordstat Yandex».

http://adwords.google.com/

http://wordstat.yandex.ru/

Click on the link and you'll see an opportunity to enter the name of a product or service, geography of distribution (Russia, Ukraine...), age of the target audience and you'll be able to "aim" at the category of customers as efficiently as possible.

Using these tools, keep in mind the question – "what will people look for when buying your product?" For example, girls who want to buy a dress, ask Google: "Where to buy a dress in Moscow?"

The most effective request will be: "Buy [product] [product model] [city]" – it is a very specific, professionally compiled request. You are especially lucky, if the request has such words as "soon" or "now".

Our goal is to discover how many people are asking about or looking for our product or service. The more there are, the better.

«Wordstat.Yandex.ru»

After opening the site, we can see the following picture:

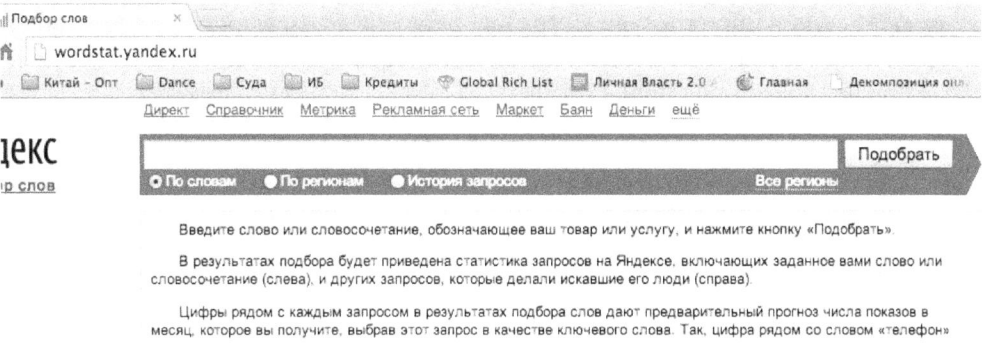

On a blank line you must enter keywords describing your product – for example, "buy a man's shirt", "buy an iPhone", "buy factory trays Kiev", etc.

It is also important to understand that requests will show statistics system Yandex.ru, and as for Ukraine, «Google» and the tool «Adwords» shall display it more accurately.

«Google Adwords»

To use this tool, you will need to register in Google. If you haven't got it yet – do it, the procedure is fast and intuitive.

After registration, you will see a page like this:

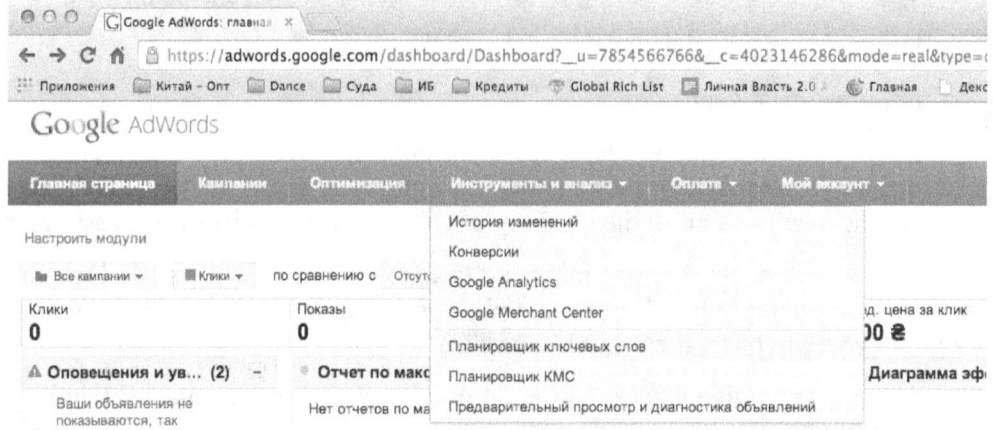

Choose "Tools and Analysis" –> "Scheduler keywords" –>"Get traffic estimates for keywords."

This is where you input your requests and get statistics on them.

Keep in mind, that Google often changing its design and at the time of reading the book, the name or link might already be changed.

Both tools will prompt the words that people are also asking when searching this product or words that are similar to your request. With their help, you will expand the number of potential customers.

Most of the CIS audience still not ready to buy products on the Internet. They have no credit cards, no accounts in the electronic payment systems, nor skills of searching for products in the online stores.

These two tools are the ways of "ejecting" preferences and identifying target audiences via the Internet. Realizing this, we can adjust the way to promote our products or services, depending on the intended niche and target audience.

Surely, you will have some more questions, but I want to remind you that our goal is to learn the trend and how the niche is demanded. At the moment, we're doing only that and nothing more.

I consider that the normal number is about 1000 and more requests per region monthly. And all of those 1000 requests are your potential customers. You can already work with such a niche – there will be enough customers. In addition, people are also looking for this product or service offline.

Picking up only 2% of the Internet market, you get 20 deals per month. If your income is $50 per unit, then such transaction volume will fully cover our required monthly plan of $1000. If the product brings you less money, then the amount of the audience should be increased.

Evaluating flow of competitors

> "Smarts come up with something, though geniuses steal"
>
> Steve Jobs

Go to the Internet or nearby shopping mall, see who else sells products you want to sell.

Come to them during business hours, and start tracking:

1. How many potential customers visiting your competitors? Mark the number of visitors per hour and extrapolate it to the entire day. There is no way out – you will have to stand still and count. Importantly, in order to be objective, take holidays, weekends and various events in the city into the account.

By the way, for the online stores there are special visitors counters (for example, alexa.com), which greatly simplifies the task.

2. What is the average sum your potential customers spend on your competitors' products? For example, I was collecting checks, which were thrown away by the visitors. This will help you understand the future profits and the percentage of people who weren't just visiting the store, but actually purchased something in it.

Sales statistics of your competitors will make your life much easier during the preparation for the opening your own shop.

Choosing a niche from offline to online and vice versa.

You can choose a niche in another way – go to the market or to the shop, which is not widely known, and see how the goods on which you want to make a bet are being sold there.

If you saw the demand for products that are not available on the Internet – congratulations, you've just found a good niche! Similarly, this mechanism works the other way – many people go to the Internet, freeing up the space in the offline.

If you can reorganize the shop from online to offline format – it's great! There will always be an audience in the market that is ready to buy in the "real" stores.

Expensive way to evaluate the prospects of niches

You can order the niche marketing analysis from specialist consultants in large companies – as in their time «Boston Marketing Group» and «Tinkoff» did.

Do you need it now? Definitely not. Invest 5-10 thousand USD in the selection of niche is meaningless: it is easier to create 5-6 projects, of which at least one will be successful. If we're talking about getting this report in the future – then definitely yes. This way you will save your time and get information from the professionals.

Search for suppliers.

There is another way – to enter the market by introducing other items, ignoring the previous steps: become a supplier's retailer, provide goods of your partners and promote it in different ways.

If by this time you have already chosen a niche, it's time to choose suppliers.

<u>We are divided by 6-7 handshakes with any man.</u>

First place, where you should look for them – your notebook. Telephone your friends, colleagues, and relatives; seek connections with people who are engaged in your niche, one way or another.

If there are any – the contacts will be provided to you. If not, ask: "Do your friends have someone, could you recommend me a man to talk to?"

This tool is strongly underestimated in the CIS. People nowadays are too afraid to talk live to each other – it is much easier to text them, send an email, etc.

Services are the same thing as production. You can sell other people's services as a commodity. It's just another business, which will provide (produce) them.

Friends are a powerful tool to resolve any issues. Do not forget about them. Use their relationships, skills, knowledge, and money.

That's how I found the "Angry Birds" soft toys (vk.com/angrytoys) and was successfully selling them. Such communication makes you closer – many of the suppliers can eventually become real friends.

The second option is to take a ride on the wholesale markets, shops, and go to other cities and countries to find places where some particular good is being already sold.

You can always start a stream with a profit of 5-10%, and after it starts, you can adjust it and find more profitable suppliers. Maybe you'll get a little profit at first, but later we will discuss how to increase it.

Today you just need to start building your shop, online store, retail outlet, etc. Find a place with goods and people, who are ready to supply you with them for resale to customers.

The third option – search an item on the Internet at eBay.com, taobao.com, alibaba.com and other sites, to find suppliers using large portals on which they are registered. At the end of the book, I have prepared a selection of sites – there you'll be able to choose your goods and suppliers.

You can always find a supplier in another country, teaming up with partners and organizing the network business. Of course, the attitude of suppliers in this case is quite different: the network business is more attractive for cooperation, because it implies greater market coverage and stable customer base.

So, we've discussed three of the easiest and fastest ways to find suppliers. Now everything depends on you – go ahead!

How to work with suppliers, having no money to purchase a product?

1. Take goods for implementation is the easiest way. You can agree that when the order comes, you take goods from the supplier or you give him an order for execution services. As for yourself, you take only the sales, customer support and product distribution.

Suppliers gladly give an item when you already have clients, but they are not so interested, if you just come with a proposal to take the goods to sell.

2. Agency contracts. You introduce the buyer to the supplier and have an interest of the transaction. In the long run this kind of business is inefficient - you immediately give away your client database and exclude yourself as a link in the business process. You need to bind the key points on yourself!

As a solution for some time, the work with the agency contracts is possible. However, there are no prospects in terms of your business development strategy.

3. Drop shipping or custom trade from another warehouse. You sell someone else's product, which is not in your physical disposal through catalogs, price lists, etc. Goods pass from the suppliers directly to the client, bypassing you.

Disadvantages of this approach lies in the fact that the supplier is in direct contact with the client, provides advertising campaign, presentation publishing, etc. You are responsible for sales only. Obviously, with this method the possibility of communication with the client is lost. And, nevertheless, it works and makes a profit.

4. Creating a sub-brand. You contact with suppliers and start to build a retail network on their behalf, using their brand. They help you with their financial and marketing resources, getting a share of the profits from trade and broad geographic distribution of their products.

Later, you can "spin-off" and develop your own network. Not every supplier can agree to cooperate in this format, but if one exists, it promises you good prospects. This option is great for starting a business.

I was making business using all the formats above, and what I've realized is one important rule: success comes with communication with people. It will help you get a unique environment for the development of your business.

Criteria for the successful niche.

How can we know whether we have chosen a successful niche?

A truly successful niche meets the following criteria:

1. Niche is clearly formulated. To whom and what we sell, what benefits it brings to the customer – this should be obvious for everyone.

2. Price at which people buy goods should be determined and meet your financial needs.

3. There is a demand on the proposed product or service on the Internet or offline, and you can satisfy some of that demand.

4. There are suppliers of products, which are suitable for operating in this niche.

5. There are first customers for this product – either in the status of potential clients, or their order is already in the preliminary stage of registration. On the Internet it will be a search requests, in the offline – questions from visitors to the store or office.

6. Orders in this niche appear fast enough, so you have the opportunity to get a bigger market share by developing your business.

You can test the 5th and 6th paragraphs, looking into the next chapter, launching the traffic, and taking advantage of free or paid advertising.

These six indicators are MY criteria of the successfully chosen niche. However, only MONEY IN YOUR POCKET is the most honest way to measure the efficiency of established business!

Conclusions:

• Your niche will answer the questions: Who are you and what do are you doing.

• Describe your target audience as detailed as you can.

• Do not be afraid to "limit" your TA – in any case, you will "catch" the others too.

• Each issue of your TA is an open door in its purse!

• Finding your niche via the Internet is much more convenient and easier.

• 1000 and more requests per month in the region is the normal quantity of potential customers to get started.

• Benefit from your connections!

• You can work with suppliers even if you have no the money to purchase goods.

Tasks:

1. Answer the questions in this chapter.

2. Write your answers very thoroughly.

3. Give your own examples.

4. Phone through your friends about interest in your product or service.

5. Walk through 50 outlets.

6. Think of 5 narrow niche products.

7. Make the analysis of competitors in your niche.

8. Check potential niches with «Yandex Direct», «Google Adwords»

9. BONUS task. Write your personal sales

Chapter 6. Launching the traffic and advertising your business

Market doesn't care from whom to buy - you or the other sellers.

Don't flatter yourself, but don't be discouraged either.

Our next chapter focuses on how to attract customers, which will bring you money. Proceed to this chapter, whenever you've chosen the niche for your business and product suppliers.

Qualitative incoming stream (QIS)

Creating QIS means creating a stream of people who will buy your product. Note – this is a stream of precisely those people, who are interested in you solving their problem!

To achieve this, we will use the methods that will be the most appropriate in your situation – the beginning of business activity.

For example, if you are going to advertise dances in high school or university, then the stream will be of the higher quality, as you work with your potential target audience. On the other hand, student advertising for ugg boots in elementary school will attract the lower quality of incoming stream of customers.

How to get a QIS?

The incoming stream of customers will become more qualitative, as more of criteria below will occur:

1. Place.

We choose places where our target audience appears – where it rests, spends its free time.

2. Desire.

The moment a person sees your ad, he – as a potential customer – must be tempted to buy the advertised product. Yes, advertising itself will motivate and "trick" the client into buying your product, but thoughtful place of its allocation or the right choice of events will greatly increase its effectiveness.

3. Money.

The person must have money to purchase your product, so that he could decide quickly. We will "lead" him on his way to purchase and help him decide to purchase.

We need advertising that meets these criteria. This will bring far greater profits in the future, because people will come already with the money and desire to buy our goods.

A good example is advertising (aka selling) sports nutrition in fitness centers or advertising windows in new buildings, real estate companies and companies of real estate developers.

How to make selling ads? Basic copywriting.

Before you the allocation place for motivating information, let's first find out how to make it sell better. Let's talk about proven ways in which our ads will give maximum results.

ODC

This model is very popular and suitable for short selling ads with volume of 3-4 sentences.

If you have a limited amount of text you can use, and you cannot describe the full proposal, this model would be an effective alternative (perfect for using in contextual advertising, on billboards, flyers, business cards, etc.).

ODC stands for:

O – offer;

D – deadline;

C – call to action.

Offer – is a kind of specific, interesting proposal that you're making to your client. Preferably, the offer should stand out among competitors' posts – thanks to the properties of the product, its benefits for the customer and a unique selling proposition.

Surely, you've noticed such advertising messages:

- *"Product with 53% discount"*
- *"Buy 1 bottle of Coke, get the second one for free"*
- *"3 for the price of 2"*
- *"Buy 3 CDs for the price of 4 and get one as a bonus"*
- *"Chairs for $9,99"* Etc.

These are the messages that simultaneously create value for the customer.

You need to choose your own offer, which will be most attractive to your customers, as well as choose the way it informs.

As for me, I found these things very efficient:

- *"The first lesson for free"*;
- *"Egypt from $149"*;
- *"Installation consultation – for free"*;

- *"Evaluator arrives the same day".*

Deadline – limitation on the purchasing of your offer. If offers' goal is to attract attention, then the deadline motivates the customer to buy right now. In other words, its goal – to make sure that people won't put off buying "for sometime later" (tomorrow, day after tomorrow, when the reason occurs, etc.), and will decide to buy your product right now.

The limit terms work very well – for example, limit of 2-3 days:

"Chairs for $9,99, just for 3 days!"

"Only until September 20th – the first lesson for free!"

Etc.

It's much easier to change the terms in the Internet. For offline advertising, it is a little harder, so the validity of offers is regularly being increased to 2-3 weeks.

Call to Action – is an explanation for the client about what he should do right now to get the desired result (buy your goods). For example:

- *"Call now and get..."*

- *"Leave your request here and we..."*

- *"Come to the store and buy..."*

- *"Tell the keyword to the seller, and get a discount..."*

Etc.

Nowadays, due to the large flow of information, you have to explain the procedure to the customer step by step. You might have noticed how effectively mandative tone in communication works.

Ordering "come here", "do this" you will see – people are willing to obey, because they don't need to fill their heads with bunch of minor things. They are happy to shift the responsibility for the decision on you!

Advertising is the same case: the clients, in fact, don't care absolutely. He needs a solution, and we give it, explaining what to do to obtain it. Simplify the task of our customers by telling how simple it is to cooperate with you!

AIDA

If you need to write a selling text or a letter, use the AIDA model. It's a method of writing the selling text based on some "checking" points or criteria, which affect the potential client.

A – "Attraction", realized in the first part of the letter. Our goal is to "hook" the customer's attention. The best ways are the screaming headline, brightly expressed offer. For example:

"7 secret ways to..."

"What is not said in the..."

"How to solve your problem?"

"What differs you from a large company?"

Etc.

Then, with the first paragraph we motivate to keep reading the text, revealing some of the "secrets", create a "trailer" for the text.

I – "Interest".

We are forming the persons' interest in your offer. You should fully describe the prospects of using your product and negative consequences if he tries to go on without it.

You can always talk about your own experience – personal example always impresses others.

It is very important in this part of the text to define the clients' benefits from buying your product. As we all know, people do not buy a drill – they need precisely drilled holes. Describe the possibilities and prospects of the client if he would make holes in the wall using your instrument!

D – "Deadline".

Already familiar to us the deadline or limitation. We artificially create a shortage of offers, consumers' excitement for your goods.

Since we have the opportunity to write a detailed text, the good thing will be to describe the reason for the deadline. Tell the customer why there is a lack of product, why the time is so limited, etc.

Deadline structure in the text can be built by answering the following questions:

- When the product will end?

- Why the product will end?

- Why you shouldn't put off the purchase?

- Why you need to buy right now?

The customer will certainly have such questions – give the complete answers in advance!

A – "Action".

What does a person need to do to buy your product right now or get a result at the same moment?

It's very good, if you give your customers a choice of three options:

1. What should a person do himself to get the same result?

2. What other place he can go to get the result?

3. How to buy your product step by step, having all the benefits from your product?

This way you are:

A – drawing attention to your product;

I – arousing interest, desire to buy your product;

D – setting a limitation on the peak of desire, so that person want to buy the product now (the deadline), and

A – explaining to the man what he has to do to get the product right now.

Pay attention to the TV show "Shop on the couch", where traders constantly use the AIDA model.

In addition, this model works perfectly for online stores, websites, direct mail and other methods of sending the informing messages to the client.

The GEVA model

This selling model is very strongly affects the emotional component of the individual – it works as great on paper, as from the mouth of the seller in your store.

Acting within the model, we actually sell the product or service to the right hemisphere of the brain of our client. The thing is to use emotions when selling a product – which, as we know, are controlled by the right hemisphere of the brain.

GEVA is another acronym that stands for:

G – Goal. Preparatory stage. We choose what goal we are pursuing, what we will describe to a person; we formulate the result, which we're trying to bring the client to.

E – Emotions. Preparatory process, the essence of which is to identify the emotion that sells goods. We're emotionally outlining all the benefits the customer will get, telling about the process of making and using our product (remember, or if you haven't seen it before, watch the presentation of "Apple" gadgets from Steve Jobs)

Bear in mind that the basic human emotions are extremely limited. In sales 6 main of them are perfectly applied:

- Fear

- Love

- Superiority

- Power

- Greed

- Pride

Once you've set a goal, selected the emotion and described the benefits for yourself, go on to the next, practical stage.

V – Visualization. At this stage, we draw a picture for client, the purpose of which is to summon the desired emotion and, at its peak, "close" the deal.

We can create a picture of the world for our customer with words, orally or in writing – the main thing that in this picture the client feels very warm and comfortable if using our product. Make sure he gets all the benefits that your product provides!

Selling text uses a lot of expressions of the following formats:

"Imagine that, feel like, realize that, hear this, look at that," etc.

Go to the next, ending paragraph:

A – Action. At the peak of emotions, we give specific instructions to the man – what he has to do right now to get our goods.

GEVA model corresponds with AIDA model, but with an emphasis on emotions and accessing them.

The text of the model is made in blocks:

1. Goal – headline and first paragraph, which installs the target.

2. Emotion – describes the key emotional state, positive or negative, the choice is yours.

3. Visualization – several blocks of text with the benefits described in a world where the customer "lives" with our product.

4. Action – describes the man what he should specifically do to get the desired product or service.

PPHS

This model has been known since the time of Socrates and is being effectively used until nowadays. This method of presentation works very well when people are hesitating for too long and cannot make a decision. I believe that PPHS is the most easily to understand the use of sales model. I advise you to pay attention!

This model is used as follows:

P – Pain. We colorfully describe to the customer what "pain" (trouble, problem, question) he has now – that exact "pain", which we are ready to relieve.

P – Pain MORE. After the first stage, we are strengthening the "pain" – thoroughly explaining what would happen if the current problem cannot be solved in the near future.

In this case, the situation is vividly illustrated by examples of the events from personal experience. Slightly modified version – you can talk about the problems in the industry and the inability to solve the problem "in the usual way."

H – Hope. At the peak of the "pain", we give the potential customer the solution – the ability to avoid it! In the mid-90s, the clichéd phrase often surfaced in advertising: "But do not despair - there is a solution!" It stuck into my consciousness, as I was a child a child – but this phrase still gives the most hope.

S – Solution. Now we sell the solution itself – describe the benefits, advantages of the goods and the method of purchase.

Now let's see how this model can be practically used, as I used it:

P:

- Why are you still fat?

- How to get rid of excess weight?

- How to learn to dance and stop looking ridiculous in a club or at the disco?

Etc.

P:

- The thicker you get, you will attract the less girls/guys!

- Education in regular schools is ineffective.

- Diets do not work.

- In 3 years of metabolic disorder, irreparable damage to inner organs occurs.

Etc.

H:

- I also encountered this problem, but found a way out!

- In fact, you're not alone experiencing the same problem!

- In such cases, there are 5 ways to solve the problem.

Etc.

S:

- *The first decision is ... the second is ... third is ... fourth is ... but there is also a fifth way, the easiest and most enjoyable ... *

- *Solution is...*

- *You can get for yourself...*

- *Make the following steps and get yourself all these benefits!*

Etc.

What to advertise? "Frontend" and "backend".

I have already mentioned these terms before, now it is time to clarify what these categories mean.

Frontend – is a "saleable" cheap goods, which promote the whole product line. We advertise it to attract the customer to our shop, where he will buys the rest.

Often, you won't earn anything or will get a very small margin on the frontend. Large companies often sell frontend as a sacrifice sale in order to attract the consumer audience. Oh, they know how much they get from a client, who will come to the shop in the future!

It is important to remember that the purpose of frontend is to attract the customer, to give him the opportunity to make the first purchase.

People have a psychological barrier: it is much harder to step from $0 to $100 purchase, than from $100 purchase to $1000 purchase. It is much easier to sell a sofa to the man, who has already bought a stool, than to a new customer.

Our task is to select a couple of positions that we promote from the entire product range. Moreover, it can be a service as well (free service, diagnostics, consultation, etc.).

Backend – it's a high margin items, those items that are most profitable to sell: they bring more money. It can be an annual subscription for the dance classes, expensive brazier of the certain alloy, etc.

Scheme to attract customers using the frontend looks like this:

- The customer comes for the advertised frontend;

- Buys frontend;

- He is being offered a specific product;

- This product is being purchased;

- Next clients' purchase is a backend (either immediately or at the 3rd -4th visit to the store).

Here you can vary the conditions. For example, fitness centers immediately "close" the purchase of an annual subscription (backend), making the offer more attractive. Typically, it includes the "free" food, sauna and other value to the customer.

On the other hand, there are businesses where managers are "touching" the client for a long time, and at the $9^{th} - 12^{th}$ touch they can sell backend. You have freedom of action, which allows you to choose your own path, based on the characteristics of your company.

What frontend to choose?

To answer this question, we stop by our competitors as "partisans", and write down all those ads with which they advertise their products or services.

If the entire market segment promotes stools, then we can go the other way: choose a small coffee table or promote services – free space measurement. If all schools offer the first lesson for free, we can offer the first lesson at a discounted price – $4,99, so to differ from the rest, etc.

In this case, it is also about solving human problems, the specific niche choosing – this particular problem we can solve better, more profitable, or just in a different way.

In order to convey our idea, we just use the methods of copywriting, which were mentioned above.

<u>Copywriting - the science, which should be studied separately</u>

In our time, there are no longer unique products. "BMW" car is just a little different from "Mercedes". Today, the main instruments in the market game are the words, product models and methods of selling them.

If the method of advertising allows us to use the photos, images, or any other visual elements, there are several options of how to use them most effectively.

1. If the image evokes the emotion that sells goods or helps purchasing.

Have you noticed that banks often hang pictures, stories that in no way relate to the financial sector?

Picture, in this case, attracts the audience, evokes those emotions that are necessary for the deal. If the grandchildren were happily running around the field, then grandmother would gladly deposit her money. If there is a young couple moving into a new apartment – people are more likely to sign a contract for a mortgage, etc. People, in this case, buy the emotion, which was installed into advertising.

2. Describing the product itself. Frankly, it is more direct and humane approach: we show the product itself, so that the client could see what he buys.

A striking example – selling electronics in the "M-Video", "Eldorado" and other giants. Follow them! Large networks are successful because they use modern techniques in sales.

Another illustration – McDonald's. Look at the burgers they sell or their published job offers. Present items in the best quality, with all the benefits, expressed in vivid colors, designs and with stunning photo angles on the packaging and success is guaranteed!

I was choosing a hotel once, which I was planning to stay in during a trip to China. One of the photos was a huge room with a large bed and flat screen TV. When I've arrived, it turned out that the hotel room is a tiny area of 3 to 4 meters, with a single bed and ... a really good plasma. That was a really well taken photo!

3. Evoking the trust. You can place yourself on the photo, your signature or a picture of famous personalities. This will help people to see you, and will help you to assure to them that you are responsible for the quality yourself and willing to speak publicly about it.

Direct mail

- *"Knock - knock"*

- *"Who's there?"*

- *"It's me, postman Pechkin, I've brought a note about your boy."*

The history of the "perfect" employee of Russian mail.

The following method is both online and offline channels of promotion. Direct mail is basically mailing. In this case, it refers to the traditional mailings or e-mail. We'll talk about the first version – mainly because just a few companies use this method.

Less than 5% of the companies in the CIS are using "direct mail" – of which, in their turn, only 5% do it qualitatively and receive a positive effect from this.

On the other hand, this method of advertising is very popular and effective in the United States. However, it has been used for so widely that this type of mailing is being literally used by every company.

Personalized mailing can begin when you will finally choose your audience and get to know your customer in person: his typical portrait, gender and location.

What you should pay attention to while organizing the direct mail?

1. You need to create, find or buy a contact list. You can use online databases, find the real addresses of the people or companies that you are interested in and make a mailing list (as an option – the express delivery for VIP-clients).

2. In order to make your campaign effective, you should write on the envelope the name of each person – the one in whose hands this letter is.

3. Letter should be decorated simply – the usual stamped envelope, sending is performed by standard post. In an envelope you put a letter with a selling text (remember copywriting techniques).

Preferably, the letter should be personalized ("Dear Alex!"), but if the financial resources or time do not give you this opportunity, then write a general statement ("Dear owner of a beauty salon", for example).

4. In a letter, be sure to specify what the customer receives, what benefits and advantages will your offer give him. Describe everything right in the selling letter – using the model of AIDA, GEVA or according to other techniques of copywriting. Write the selling text on 2 or 3 A4 sheets and sell your product or service to a specific person.

5. Count payback. If your item with a price tag of less than $5 and you have no expensive products for sale, do not complicate your life with direct mail – it will be just unprofitable.

6. Aim for a series of letters. Your task is to send not one, but three letters to each of the clients. The first one will give you about 2% of responses, and the second one about 5-7%, and the third will "push" to 13%. In this case, you should always notice the item in the letter, which people react more to, what text sells better and what percentage of letters reach their destination.

7. Frequency. Do the mailing today, send the following letter a week later, the second one – in two weeks, and then check the results. Repeat mailing campaign every 1-3 month, changing some elements of appeal and selling text.

8. Use outsourcing. Mailing can be delegated to someone else – there are special companies that are specializing in direct mail (use Google for details).

It is better to run the first campaign on your own – in the first place, you need to measure the return on it. Second, the current level of professional direct mail companies in the CIS is not high enough, they simply cannot do a profitable campaign on their own, from scratch.

If your direct mail campaign goes "zero" or goes to an acceptable "minus", which may be covered by the profits from the backend, you need to keep it for sure! New customers, whom you will receive, will bring a lot more money.

9. The effectiveness. In order to make the receiver open your letter, and not throw it out in the trash, put one of the things below inside your envelope:

- Coin, $1(ruble, the rupee - on your choice);

- Aspirin;

- Key, nut;

Etc.

I personally experienced this – so did the real professionals of direct mail. When the recipient receives the envelope, inside of which there is an attachment, he is interested in discovering what it is and why it is there. In addition, this is an excellent opportunity to "attract" the potential client with the words:

- "Do you know why I've put here an aspirin? I want to save you from headaches, it's time to..." and so on.

<u>Act according to the AIDA model – attract customers and arouse interest</u>

The product you sell also influences increase of the efficiency of mailing. Better if it is your frontend.

To further explore this method of advertising, read Dan Kennedy. The book is called "Selling letter" – one of his best works on direct mailings.

Let's analyze the question on the example of the western guru, if you want to get examples of letters and my essay on it – send me an e-mail: jtc.audit@gmail.com, I'll be happy to send you those.

The email-mailings are carried out according to the same principles as direct mail – only in online format, without envelopes and attachments.

There are many services on automating e-mail-lists. The most popular and convenient are:

- Justclick.ru

- Smartresponder.ru

- Mailchimp.com

And many others – look for all the information about them on the Internet.

Go to these websites, sign up – to start mailing free versions will be suitable. This will help you to constantly communicate with your audience.

Contacts of your potential customer base is easy to find on the Internet – often they are freely available and can be bought from vendors, but the most effective way is **to collect contact information on your site**.

There are special plug-ins – for example we'll take a look at the **popup Domination**, which I use myself. The developers site has different versions and so there will be the one, suitable for your website.

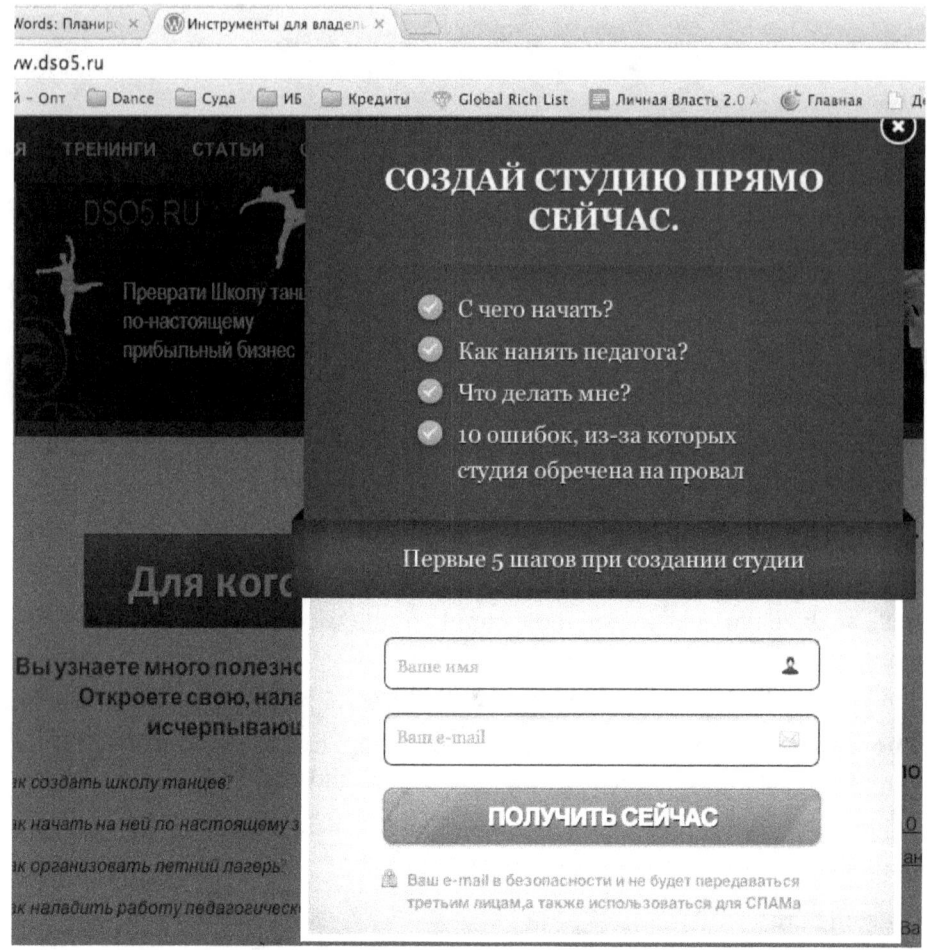

As you can see - application allows you to collect contacts directly from the site, in addition to email and name, it is also possible to add phone / city and other if necessary.

Also, you should collect customer contacts in your offline retail outlet – so you will make your base for the mailing.

Preparing and sending 500-600 letters took me one day.

Then I started to use the services of freelancers or students – for 10-15 dollars they signed envelopes, indicating name, zip code and address.

Now I order printed letters in the copy center or in companies that specialize in direct mail. They print and personalize each letter. It costs a little more, but the quality is much higher - in addition, I am really saving my time.

Summary: direct mail - a very good way to advertise, I recommend it for services and goods, which cost more than 50 dollars.

Calculate all of the costs and potential profit – maybe for you direct mail would be an appropriate option for selling even cheaper products.

Partnership programs

This method is applicable not only to the Internet format of doing business, but also quite successfully used doing things "in the real world". In the category of "partner" get businesses or people who can sell your product.

Such schemes are often used in the automotive business, paying interest for attracted customers. Modern Russian Info business also full of partnership offers.

Qualitatively launched partnership program - when people are making profit by selling your product - can provide you with 20-30% or more of total sales, depending on the type of business.

You need to find a company or people who will be willing to enter a partnership program and input your goods in a catalog or on a showcase. You can ask to use their client base – in this case, your ability to communicate with your customers will increase dramatically!

It's always more pleasant to work with partners – often it is a business, interested in profits from new products. **In fact, it's your sellers, who work for you, but do not get anything in return, except for interest from the future sales, which are not here yet.**

In this case, they already have a contact database that will provide a stream of clients (not one-time transactions, but literally the stream of customers).

If your business is located in the Internet, look there for the partner database, sites similar to justclick.ru, clickbank.com. You can also team up with other businesses or online stores via the Internet.

You can either compete with shops, or you can help each other. The second option suits me more. Competition is good, it gives people a choice. So why not earn on it? This possibility opens using partnership programs.

In general, "parasitizing" on the partner client base – it's a great way to quickly promote your product.

I hired workers who were selling my range of goods - they were running to the shops and school to sell my services and products. Websites were in the role of "sellers" of my services on the Internet.

I combined my store of soft toys with dozens of other children's stores. In fact, I was the only owner of those toys (they were lying on my suppliers' stock), but, nevertheless, pictures of these products were in the catalogs of my partners, each of which was regularly selling something.

Internet advertising

Announcements boards.

This category includes sites such as slando.ru, torg.ru, freetorg.ru, avito.ru, ria.ua and other sites with **free posting of advertisements**.

It's quite effective to place ads on them – especially using the ODC-model we have talked about (look offer, deadline, and call to action).

A huge advantage of such sites is that the service of posting is free of charge and all the boards are well indexed (they are very easy to find at the request with Yandex and Google).

We place our products wherever possible: preferably - one ad = one product. People visit sites, looking, buying – you can easily see how it's done yourself.

On many sites, in order to raise the position of your ad you have to pay a weekly fee. Alternative free way - you can simply delete the ad, and then post it again. My partner, for example, simply instructed his employees to periodically remove and post these ads again.

Ads structure for free "boards"

To make your ads sell more effectively, I'll give a little explanation of their structure. By following these recommendations, it will be much easier to make a deal.

1. **Strong title**, offer.

We make a strong headline - it's not just a "product", "quality product", "super toy" or "toy for the children". It should attract the attention: "Top of Sales", "How to have fun?" "Present this toy to your kid", "Hit among buyers", "Discount product", etc.

2. **Emotional hook.**

This means that we have to "hook" the man into reading our text. As an example - present the real information on our behalf: for telephone it can be formulated as follows: "Telephone from the world champion" or "Telephone that saved my life", etc.

3. **Emotional description**.

Tell them how you used this phone, why it's so cool, how it rescued you, etc. Give specific, personal description of this product, emphasizing how cool to use it. Tell about how it is pleasant to hold in your hands, describe how stylish the buyer will look with it, etc.

4. **Photos.**

Use the professional (from the site or portal of producer) and amateur (take a picture of the package, the product or the customer, who received the order) photos.

It seriously increases the trust of potential clients to you – they have the confidence that this product is not just "somewhere", but in the stock.

5. **The reason for selling**.

Indicate why you sell this product – due to your trading campaign, a new shipment or anything like that. It will be easier for person to buy if there is the justification for himself, the answer to the question: "Why now? Why this particular product?"

6. **Benefits**.

We describe the emotional and real, physical benefits of the product. Comparison with competitors, with an indication of the benefits of your product will work very well.

This technique is clearly illustrated in the sites of manufacturers of sports nutrition. They always compare themselves with competitors using the table with the criteria that are beneficial for them. Example - http://bodybuilding.com/ - use it as a role model!

7. **Rewards**.

You shouldn't economize on this one! You can specify that some small bonus comes with a product, an accessory or a free course - describe what a person will get "on top" of his purchase. This way you raise the value of the product with the bonus, which will also attract customers.

Internet advertising: banners, teasers.

The next paragraph on our advertising marathon – the Internet advertising in two formats: banners and teasers. In fact, they are built on the same principle – the desire to click on the picture. Accordingly, they appear on the screen as a picture and different pop-up windows.

Our goal in using these banners – create the right context.

In this case, we can divide the entire audience into two categories of people, and two ways to approach them.

The first category: the person who is looking for something, exploring specific sites, he has a desire to satisfy his need or solve a problem. And that is what he's looking for on the Internet.

The second category: people surf Internet, aimlessly clicking on different sites for entertainment.

In both cases, our teaser advertisements start selling goods, so to speak, "straight ahead".

It is understood, that this type of advertising is working with extremely small CTR (click-through rate) – you should work to maximize the number of impressions (up to a million impressions per day).

The aim is the person clicking on the banner and going to your website. Next you either start "lead" him to purchase, or leading him to inputting his contacts.

The cost of such advertising is very cheap - but also the incoming audience is of poor quality. The main advantage of such advertising is a low cost and a large number of impressions. Personally, I use services such as Marketgid.com, Begun.ru и Click.ru.

Of course, all text information should be prepared in the format of the ODC – this is what I have already mentioned several times.

Internet advertising: YD and GA. Contextual advertising

YD and GA stand for "Yandex Direct" (direct.yandex.ru) and "Google Adwords" (adwords.google.com).

These are two services of contextual advertising. Their principle of operation is that the people in these search engines by typing in their requests receive information about your products and services together with the found references – of course, if your niche matches with the request.

I won't explain you the process of signing up, I'm sure you're able to understand everything on your own. Startup process looks like this:

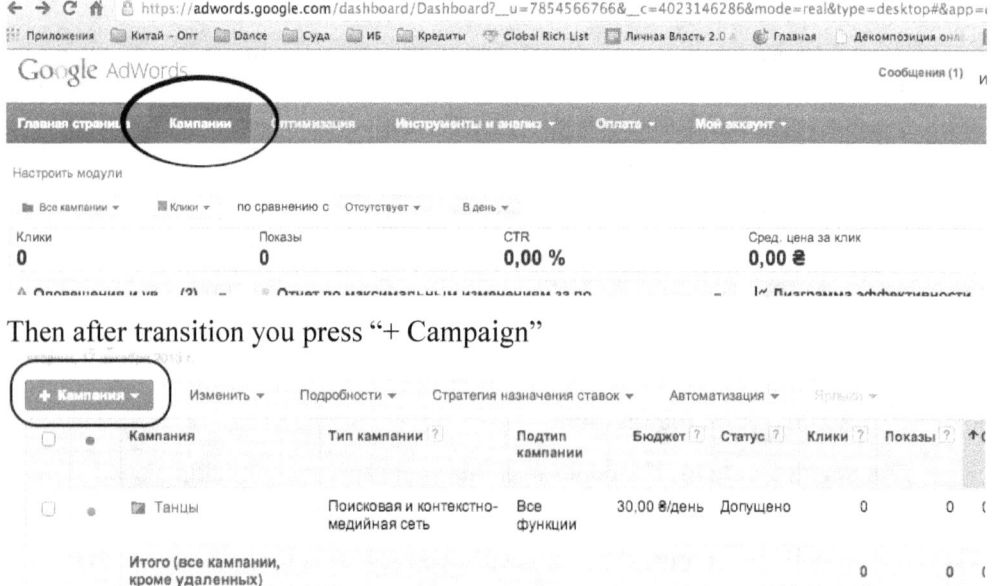

Then after transition you press "+ Campaign"

In the drop-down menu – choose to start with, «search network only» – it will be easier to track down and understand the results.

Then leave everything as standard in the fields.

Fill only the estimated budget. The following window will appear:

Then fill in the fields, everything is intuitive, you can play with it for a little bit, but let's clarify using the ODC:

- Title - Main title - offer

- Description row 1 - help to the offer + call to action

- Description row 2 - deadline

- Displayed URL - enter the starting page of the site here

- Target URL - here we type in that product's page, which will refer to the ad.

Play for a while, type in the text in these values and you will understand how they work, the good thing is that it shows the changes in real time on the right.

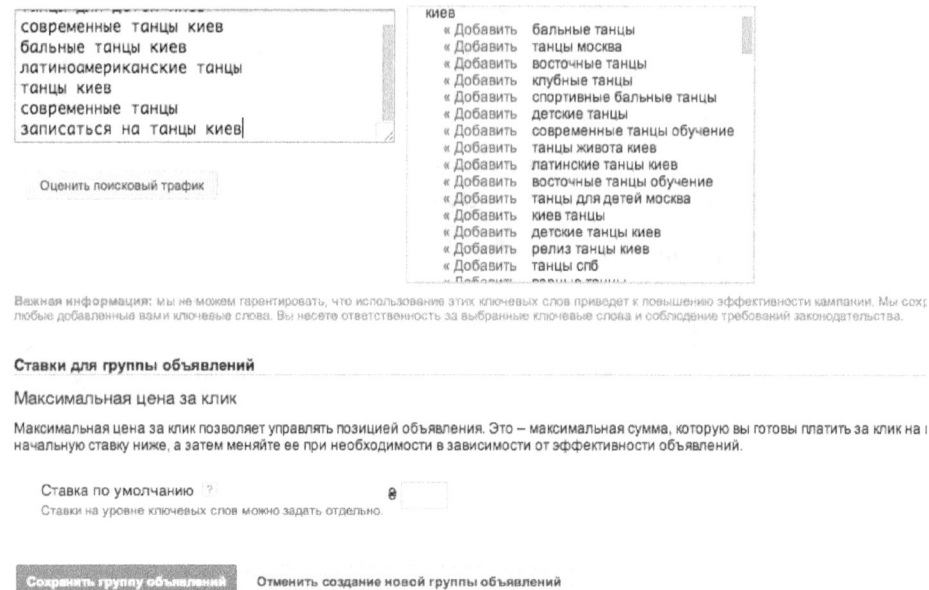

At the bottom you enter keyword values - those requests for which your ads will pop-up, and the default rate is the price for one click.

Remind yourself the chapter above.

Now a little about Yandex:

Go to the website:

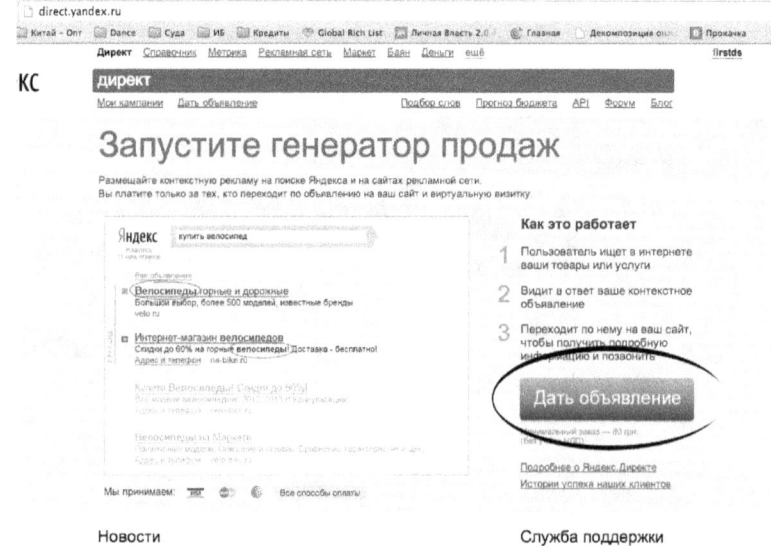

Then skip the page – leave it as it was (if you are not specialist, of course), because, by default, your region and coverage, etc., are configured; go to the step 2, "Giving an advertisement"

Here, similar to Google, we enter Title – offer.

Advertisement text – an explanation for the offer, the deadline, and a call to action, enter the link and key requests. Everything is simple and similar to the method from Google Adwords described above.

Now we only have to enter the price, how much we are willing to pay for people clicking on our advertisement. The principle is simple – the more we put, the more impressions we get, and the faster we run out of clicks.

In order to configure everything more professionally you should talk to the specialists. I have described the basic level.

KEY FEATURE: In these two methods, we can choose an already created context, the circumstances in which a person is looking for a solution, ready to buy our products. Contextual advertising systems allow us to find these people, "hook" them and start selling.

The main essence of the contextual advertising – the limit of 3-4 lines, so use the ODC model and place an ad with a link.

* Study the TARGET CALL function or SPOOFING the phone number (Yandex function) - this will help you to measure advertising effectiveness.

Internet advertising: SMM, VK, FB

The next sphere of Internet advertising is SMM – Social Media Marketing, or the promotion of your product through social networks, such as "VKontakte" and "Facebook".

These two social networks are perfect for the start of sales. After you can add "renren.com" (Asia), "YouTube" and others – but this would require a more advanced level of you.

What promotion tools do you have in social networks?

Photo albums – it's your products' catalog. Personal Messages – personalized correspondence. Mailing to subscribers – direct mail. Use your minds' flexibility and you'll understand!

Options of doing business in a social network:

1. You can sell through your profile directly from your page. Subscribed customer base, "cold" contacts – these are your friends and subscribers. They are easy to work with if you post the news of your life.

The selling page looks like this:

Under the button "add to friends" you'll see your friends (these people are doomed to read your spam and selling texts☺).

2. You can sell through the group.

Create a group for desired topic; make people go there with the help of advertising in other communities or targeting (described later).

4. You can also create and maintain the "public group" and sell through it.

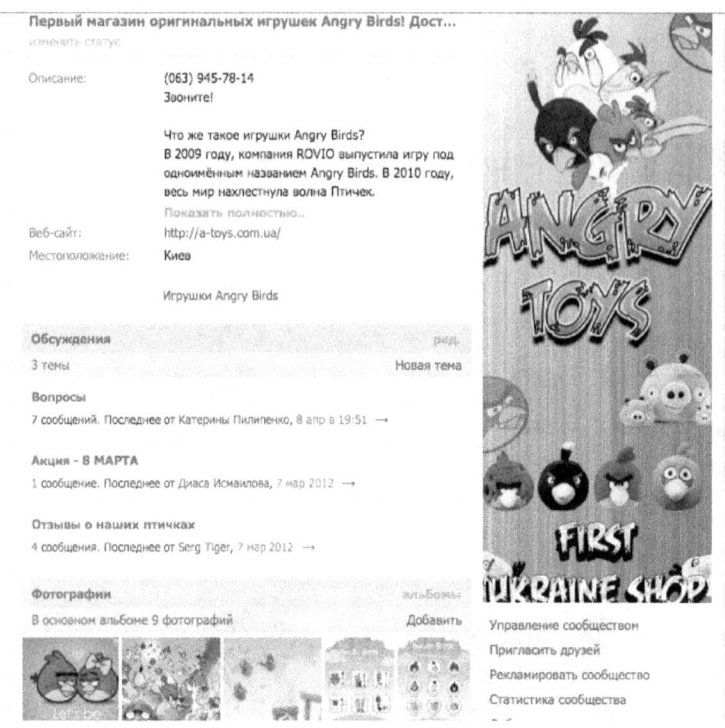

Theoretically, when working in social networks the number of purchases is limited only by your capabilities for the shipment of goods, as in these two social networks – "VK" and "Facebook" –a huge number of professionals are working. They can get you dozens of subscribers and build a sales scheme at a reasonable price.

If you want to organize everything by yourself, just add 40 new friends per day – it is the minimum required amount of new contacts for regular sales. And sell to each of them personally. Communicate using scripts (see below), work with the objections and sell / sell / sell. As soon as you'll create a stream, you'll be able to delegate.

In networks there is a special and targeting advertising that is designed for a specific target audience. While it is relatively cheap – use it to sell your goods. How to do it? Just go to the Advertising section – in the contrast to the above-described methods, it is difficult to make a mistake here.

And the same as above:

Title – the main, screaming offer.

Description – an explanation, deadline and a call to action.

Notice, that in the VK (like in a Facebook), you need to add a picture that allows you to create the right atmosphere and visualize the product – use it.

After preparing your ad, you have to enter the targeting data – you choose to whom it will be shown and the price.

That's it, start now, it will be checked by the moderators (it takes about 15 minutes) and the clicks stream will begin.

A few words from a partisan.

What other nuances are able to increase the efficiency of you advertisements?

- Discover other social networks: LinkedIn, Profeo, Google+, etc. It is a place where people haven't yet learnt how to sell, so the advertising market is empty. You can be number one.

- Business cards can be placed in the window of the driver. Often, people who have already mentioned them, take a look what is left for them. At the same time, putting my business cards in the books in stores, the method I've read somewhere, never worked for me.

- Partner sales. This type of sales proved to be the most effective for me. I took the goods of my partners and sold it at my place – they did the same – and as a result, both variants brought huge profits. Do not miss this opportunity to earn!

- Flyers can bring your "under-competitors" – businesses that still do not compete with you, but in the long term they can. If your business is a manicure, bring your flyers to the barbershops in your neighborhood, while they're not providing this service, but in the nearest future they would be happy to do that.

Walk with your flyers through all the companies that are in your district – we'll talk about the **map of the area** later on, you can Already leave the "wastepaper" to your partners for the distribution.

- If your neighbors or competitors organize competitions, exhibition or conference, do not miss the chance to place there the information about yourself – just bring your flyers and spread them out on tables.

I remember as one of the events that I organized had the flyers of my competitors. Of course, they were immediately thrown out, but part of my audience yet received an offer from another company. I was terribly angry, argued with them – but they got their results anyway.

Conclusions:

• In order to increase the number of customers coming because of your advertising and bought goods, you must place your ads in the area where your TA is, where they have a desire to buy and have the money to do it.

• Study copywriting – this will help to raise the conversion of mailings.

• Use direct mail for "personal" impact on the target audience.

• Frontend often unprofitable but attracts customers.

• To stimulate sales organize various events – promotions, discounts, etc.

• Increase the value of flyers.

• Use services of freelancers more often and you can save on the creation of mailing.

• Social network – the place to attract cheap customer

Tasks:

- Preform each of the described methods of advertising.

- Write three selling texts (short, full and trim-full).

- Place an ad in the 20 free announcement boards.

- Get at least 200 potential customers.

- Deal with the function of the target call and start to keep records – from where and how many clients you get.

Chapter 7. Conversion and Convertors

> *"We will conquer this city, but not many people will return home ... This is the price of freedom!"*
>
> Fragment of speech before the battle

What is a "conversion"?

Conversion is Latin translation for transformation. In terms of our goals, we will consider the conversion as a transformation of your potential customers into active ones.

Convertor is a platform that organizes the conversion, thanks to which the sale itself takes place.

What can be a converter?

Converter can be:

- Website;

- Your hired seller;

- The store itself;

- Your office;

- Some alternative ways of presenting your products and services.

Now we'll take a look at these five points – when you'll realize the principle, it won't be difficult for you to select the suitable converter. Next, you measure the data and monitor the dynamics – the most effective tool we will need to bring to perfection.

For the rapid increase in sales the highest potential cash enclosed in these convertors. For example, through advertising you've got about 500 people to your store from which only 10 made the purchase. This way, your conversion is now 2%, while raising it from 2% to 4%, you increase your sales by 2 times.

Often, the proper placement of selling triggers and motivational materials on these platforms allows you to raise profits by 2-3 times. All of this can be done at almost no cost, and most importantly – very quickly, in contrast to, for example, a symmetric double increase of advertising budget.

You choose what is better for you to do right now. You can just carefully analyze your website – look, good or bad it is made, how do people behave coming to it – are they leaving or staying.

You can upgrade another convertor – try to teach your dealer how exactly he has to sell. If you sell yourself, then try to teach yourself the correct plan of actions, looking in the mirror, etc.

Whatever it will be, in order to build the fundamental mechanism of sales and an acceptable level of conversion, you'll have to carefully study this chapter.

Purpose of the website.

Let's start with the goals of your site. Understand one thing – the website is used for selling your services. It should not inform, should not improve your image, should not increase your presence on the Internet – it should only sell!

<u>The only purpose of the website is to increase sales</u>

You can use the site as a "frontend" – it can increase your customer base, which you then will SELL TO.

It can be done directive (selling directly in the forehead, for example, with the help of an online store) – a man comes with established need and buys the necessary good from you at once.

Another option is to sell using the "touch": for example, do the "landing page" and put the ordering module on it. A man leaves his application to purchase, then there is its processing (call or e-mail to the client), and then the purchase itself.

Remember, if you're ordering the website from an agency, carefully study the nuances of its structure. Perhaps they will say, "we'll make you a beautiful design, we will do this and that..." – not worth listening to, because the main goal for us is to SELL! You have to explain what they should do by yourself.

How to effectively explain what do you want to the programmer or a designer?

There is a special program called "Balsamiq Mockups". With its help, you can draw a pattern layout of your future site, which will be taken as a basis by a programmer and designer.

How to save money on the development of the website?

Break it up into 3 phases to create and perform each separately. Saving on each will allow you to save overall.

Stage 1 – the creation of design. With "Balsamiq Mockups" you've traced the pattern and gave it to the designer. From him you will receive the Photoshop .psd file in "layers".

Stage 2 – typesetting. The stage at which the website is transformed from a static picture into a "living organism". For a simple website, work ends here, and the coder puts it on the Internet.

Stage 3 – programming. The goal is to make everything work on your website exactly as you need: titles are highlighted and flashing, clues are popping-out when you need them, the proper message is generated when you go to another page, etc.

If your site will use the CMS system ("Content Management System", google it), do not get lost in doubt – choose any. It will bring you the necessary usability features of the site, and at the beginning it is more than enough.

Do not overpay for CMS! If you will need to seriously modify it, just recruit professional who will realize all your wishes, based on a comprehensive analysis.

Template scheme of the selling "landing page"

We'll start with the most simple and common conversion platform – your website.

Now you're just getting into the business, but if you fulfilled the tasks of the preceding chapters, then you've already have 1 or 2 successful products or services. In order to sell them, you will have to use a tool such as Landing page. I've said about it before, and now we look at the principles of creating this page in more detail.

What is it?

Landing is one landing page, the purpose of which is the sale of a particular product, or receiving an order for its purchase. No more useful functions for the visitors on this page, so you limit a person in his choice.

How should the Landing look like to increase sales?

To do this, we will examine its scheme by several blocks, each of which is dedicated to its particular purpose.

1. At the top, we put **the main title**, which should "hook" the client. It can be a phrase, like "some goods with a discount", "solution to the painful problem" or "offer of anything to you, dear customer".

Remember copywriting, remember previous selling texts models – use your imagination and logic!

2. Be sure to put your **number** at the top. This should be done at all times! Write it in big letters, add an explanation – how and when they can reach you (for example, 24/7, or from 15.00 to 15.30 GMT). Explained that if any questions occur they need to call this number.

3. In the middle of the top part, you must indicate **a slogan, a picture** on the topic, etc.

4. Below you put a form of subscription and, if you are capable of it, a video or an explanation to the product: an audio or video message, in extreme cases, this may be a photograph or illustration. In the form of subscription, customers indicate their phone, e-mail and name.

I should note that it is a video message that works best.

5. Go on – after the subscription form you put **3 blocks: the "Guarantees" block, the "Benefits" block and the "Delivery" block** with built-in icons and text.

You can modify them, put something in, something out – but the guarantees block (100% refund if the client is unsatisfied) should be placed carefully: so we remove the most important objection of the individual – the risk of the purchase.

Block "Guarantees" contains information about the subject of your warranty, and with what you are responsible for your actions (100% match of originality, 100% refund, etc.).

Block "Benefits" describes the main reason to buy from you now (discounts, sales, quality, originality, etc.)

Block "Delivery". If you are to provide services, it is possible to explain exactly how your company is doing it, what progress had been made, etc.

6. Any person while reading the page will **unavoidably encounter with objections** of any kind. Therefore, as a tool for their removal, we provide **reviews** of other people who have already bought your product.

If you still don't have such reviews – ask your friends of a little favor: let them act as your customers, collect their "stories of using" your services or products. If you have regular customers, ask them to leave a comment and be sure to put it within this block.

7. Go down even lower and make **an overview of the technical side** – describe the characteristics of the products. If it is a service, please indicate how the process of its delivery is being preformed, and which technology is being used. Briefly tell them exactly what will happen or what kind of a product person is going to buy.

8. Then there are **the benefits** of working with you. Here you describe 5-7 typical problems byers face with while working with your competitors. These are the main objections that need to be worked out, the objections that people face using your product.

It may be a problem with the prices, the delays, poor quality of goods, problems with service or delivery, etc.

And, you have to immediately follow with specifying the reasons why they need to choose only you. Of course, there should be more reasons – at least 10-12. Those may be direct delivery, fast order processing, etc. – indicate the reasons of a different order.

9. Paragraph №4. Repeat it 2-3 times as scrolling down the Landing.

10. **Optional.** We have already pointed out the basic information about with which we have worked, have shown how it works, we pointed out the reviews, reasons for and against making a purchase. Further, we can insert another form –

for wholesale buyer ("If you want to buy a lot of products – leave your contacts here").

If your product is quite expensive, you can insert a block of your legal entity – with the details, contacts, and all the necessary information. People need to understand – your product is expensive, and you won't disappear without a trace with their money.

11. Landing ends with possible **ways of payment for purchase and a description of the delivery process.**

End the page with one more subscription block – see paragraph №4.

A great example of Landings:

http://ideo.su/steb/

http://bmhostel.ru/

http://land.dso5.ru

Moving on. The most interesting part is online stores. It is a website, attending which a customer purchases a product right there. If using Landing we collect contacts or sell a particular product, in the online store a person chooses from a large range of products the one that he wants.

Quite a lot of "tricks" are known in sales for online stores, there is a lot of speculation, a lot of proven technologies to increase sales. Now I'll tell you about those, which I have personally tested – we'll do it in the form of a website review that has proved its effectiveness.

Home page.

Take a sheet of A4, draw two horizontal and two vertical lines. You get 9 squares – simple and clear matrix. We start with the upper left corner.

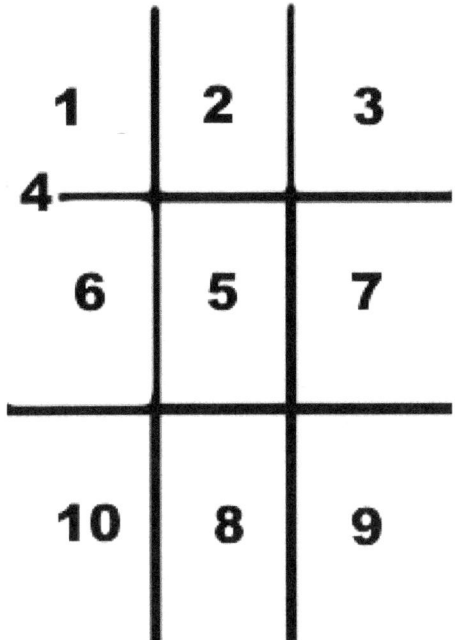

1. **Descript**. Here (in the upper left corner) we specify the name of your company. If it is unavailable or you just started your work, do not waste time on mega-creative thing: simply enter the name of the site.

For example, if your customer comes to your website that sells erotic costumes, it would be specified as the "ero-costume.com.ua. Erotic costumes with delivery in Ukraine".

Descript formula can sound as follows – "This is a convenience store with delivery across the country, across Russia, across Ukraine, across the world, across America and so on".

2. **Logo.** In the middle of the top part, you put a logo or an image that relates to the subject of your website. When a person comes to the store, he looks, if he got where he needed, read the description of the website – for example, spare parts for motorcycle – and sees the corresponding illustration at the top. It becomes clear that he came where he wanted, and he can continue exploring the site.

3. On the right top part you put the **phone number** using the large font and input the "**Order the callback**" button. If the customer clicks on it, the corresponding form pops up, where he can leave his contact information and your manager (or you yourself) will contact him later.

4. Next is a horizontal line – the separation of several blocks, **the buttons panel**. It should have links such as:

• "Home page", so a person could always go back to it.

• "Catalog". Button name should be like that – not "List of products", not "Products", but namely the "Catalog": I can say from personal experience, it works much more efficiently.

• "Reviews", clicking on which, a person goes to a page with reviews of cooperation with your company.

• "Shipping and payment" – your client needs to know exactly how is he able to pay for and receive his products.

• "Contacts" – how to find your company.

• And, if necessary, add "FAQ" and "About Us". These pages serve as a kind of supplement to the basic structure of the site where a person can find the answers to the questions that he asks most often (suppliers, achievements, access to discounts, etc.).

5. Move to the second row – the central window. This is **a big action** – the product name for the implementation of which we do the current marketing event. Big picture, big letters, big discount and a small slider. Text, for example, might be: "discount on the most popular clothing", "discount on shirts just today", etc.

6. On the left in the middle row, we specify the familiar **3 blocks – "Guarantees", "delivery", "benefits"**.

Their separation is conditional and you can vary their location as you wish. Why are they needed? Re-read the section "Landing page".

7. Next – middle row on the right. Here we place the **"Catalog",** which will allow people to click on the correct place directly from the home page.

8. Go to the middle of the bottom row. Enter here the most popular types of goods – the ones that customers buy most willingly. Specify them as much as possible to the bottom of the page.

A little secret – to the related image of the goods must be attached sale icon or symbol "top sales", etc. "Buy" button should lead to such a product directly from the home page. Submit at least 25-30 such products until the end of the page.

9. Bottom row, the cell on the right – these are **customer reviews,** those people who have already bought something from you. It may seem like a small strip with the reviews texts and pictures. It is very good, if there are be also reviews posted in audio and video format, supplementing the standard text. This is a very effective method to increase customer confidence in your online store.

10. Lower cell on the right – **free block**. One of the options to use it is to put there a **subscription form, some bonus to your customers for leaving their contacts**. In fact, it can be anything, whatever you want.

You can make a pop-up window that appears when a person comes to your site, with the following content: "Leave your request and you will be constantly informed of all our events" or "Get a discount on your first purchase", etc.

11. Put another small descriptor containing just a couple of lines in the bottom of the website: the name of the store and the organizational and legal form (SP, Ltd.).

12. **WARNING!** At the end of each page should be the "go to the next page" button. It's very uncomfortable to scroll up to the beginning every time – because of this, some customers may just leave your store.

You can make the "jump to the top" button or pop-up window and go-back button – or you can add one more button below. If people did not find anything, then you use it simply to get the client back to the catalog.

When a customer opens a catalog and scrolls it to the end, you send him to the reviews. From there – again the catalog, etc. The logic of movement on your website should be well elaborated!

Usability of your online resource increases the depth of the showing and time the person stays on the website. Accordingly, your store will be displayed in the search engines at higher positions.

From the buyers' point of view– if he has not found all that he needed, and then you continue to communicate with him, **"taking him to another show-room."**

13. **"JivoSite" and others**. The site at the bottom of each page (or any other suitable place) should have the "Order the expert consultation" button. If a person has a question when purchasing a product, and there is no one to ask about it, the deal could be derailed.

Bear in mind that this is also an active working with clients, and due to its good organization, the conversion can grow from an average of 1-5% to 40%!

"Catalog" section and product page.

What should you pay attention to except the home page?

What is the difference between such pages as "FAQ", "Contacts", etc.?

1. When you open them, you leave the "hat" and the right block on their place, be sure to leave reviews, changing only the main, central part of the window.

2. You change the main action on "FAQ", "Contacts" or conditions of delivery and payment, depending on the page.

3. I remind you that on the end of each page you place the button, clicking on which the visitor can go to the "Catalog", "Reviews" and so on in order to allow the visitors move further in the exploring of your site at the end of the page.

Now I insist on studying the "catalog" in more details – there is a lot to talk about.

What will this page consist of? Besides the fact that we leave all those blocks that go through the whole site (see above), we make a small description of the page, followed by the separation of its subdirectories.

Each such subsection should insert a photo and title. For example, if we are talking about spare parts of the car, the title can look like: "for the engine", "for the cabin", "for the car", etc. Then, after the list of subdirectories, you place the button of purchase again to let the client buy the product if he wants to.

You can also insert the random products that will randomly alternate, while providing a full catalog of products in the ordered list.

If a person clicks on a subdirectory (for example, he chose the spare parts for the engine), it opens a list of these parts.

If you have just a few products, removing the subdirectories can substantially reduce the size of your catalog.

Once a customer clicks on any item there opens **the product, i.e. selling page.**

What is necessary to specify in it?

This page should contain:

1. **Several big photos of a good quality**, one of which is presented in expanded form, and the rest are located side by side in the form of miniatures. Each of them has the ability to be enlarged – when you press on it (for example, photos of product from different angles, etc.)

2. **Emotional product description** in simple language. For example, this refrigerator is specially designed for large families, it can be bought in several color variations, it has the following advantages, etc. For example, you can specify: "Two cameras will help you keep the vegetables in a suitable temperature and enjoy good products even after 2-3 hours of the absence of electricity, and so on".

3. **Technical description.** Specifies the full explanation in the volume of 2-3 paragraphs: the size, capacity, power consumption, variations in shape, color, size, etc.

4. **Price.** Specify the price: the "old" – crossed out, near the lower new price. When this particular product is without action, you should just indicate the price, but always using **LARGE FONT**! Make sure that each product has the price tag – it is very important from the point of view of the image of the online store.

5. **Objections**. Here we specify the problems that typically arise when buying products from competitors, or order services. Write down what you should

look for when making a purchase, what problem is most likely to occur and what are the benefits for the buyer when buying it from you (in a ratio of 5 problems, 10 benefits).

6. **The "Order" button**. Placed at least 2 times – the first time after the item description, the second time after working with objections, at the very bottom of the page.

7. Next to the "Order" button, you put the already familiar "**Order the expert consultation**" button – a person can click on the button to leave his contacts, and you or your manager will call him and answer his questions.

Social Networks – creating the sales platform

Another place where you can create your own website analogue and sell with it – the social network.

If you sell all over the world, including Asia, then you will be interested in such little known websites for a wide range of Russian Internet users as "RenRen", "QQ", etc. If you are guided primarily by the West, I recommend the "Facebook". If your target audiences are the CIS countries, the perfect choice would be "VKontakte".

Now I will talk about the general principles that should be considered when selling through social networks.

Regardless of the selected network, conditions are practically the same.

1. The first thing from which the communication with the client begins is a kind of "avatar" – the "face" of the company. Post the logo of an online store and a small descriptor (description), i.e. proceed with a similar online store design technology.

Specify the website – in this case it will be the name of the group and an explanation in the familiar format ("... shop, with delivery" and themed picture on the background). You also put your contact information for communication here.

2. In the central block (above the menu), you post a general description, which will contain the type of activity, the benefits of co-operation with your company, work experience and a link to the website along with the phone number.

3. Graphical menu. Again, act by analogy with the design of the site – in particular, place the panels with links to the catalog, home page, "FAQ", "About us", etc.

4. You have the ability to add links on the right – you can paste the "Our Community" link there, so a man not only could join the group, but also subscribe to the Public – newsfeed of your business. Here you can also give the coordinates of your website.

What should I create – a group, a page or a public?

This issue is relevant for "VKontakte", because in "Facebook" and other foreign analogues everything is intuitive.

If earlier in the "VK" you could create a page (individual account), create its profile and sell through it, now you can do business only through the group. If your personal "selling" page will be spotted, you won't be able to avoid the ban.

Thus, the group should be created as a shop, public – for the news of your business and "direct mail".

5. In the "Discussions" section, you post the FAQ, customer reviews (they should also be placed on the main wall and published in the discussions).

6. In the lower right corner of the page, give a link for communication with managers.

7. Then, in the photo album, you post the information about products ("**Catalog**"), in a video section you put the overview videos for products or thematic videos.

Therefore, you can create a complete online store in "VKontakte", which can be made quickly and cheaply. The only things, which you would have to work on, are the graphical menu and division into subdirectories (albums), but no problems should arise here.

Convertor: seller - phone.

Next convertor is your seller, the person whom you have left to work directly with clients, whether it the cold calling or personal selling. The administrator also falls into this category.

Seller – is the person who changes potential customers into the active ones, and this what makes him a convertor himself.

What should I pay attention to?

Look at the three criteria:

- The appearance of the seller;

- What he says;

- How he says.

I think, no question should arise about the appearance: the seller must look neat and tidy, in accordance with the dress code of your company. However, on **what he says and how he says,** we will take a closer look.

How he says?

I will give a couple of recommendations on this subject.

1. Before he begins to ring up the customers, the person needs just to smile, in order to make his voice more pleasant. Customers feel the warmth of communication and, consequently, buy much more willingly.

2. Often, sellers begin to chat on the phone with the position of "bottom-up". It is fundamentally not right. Your task is to position yourself on the same level with the client. You should build up the sellers speech based on this – the manager should say in a pleasant, calm voice and communicate with the client on an equal footing.

What he says?

1. If a person calls with "a hook" (had a previous contact, recommendation, etc.) or "coldly", the speech script is structured in such a way:

- "*Hello*", then comes the question: "*This is the ... company, Sergei?*"

and we are **waiting for a response from the man**.

If he says, "yes, it's me" (if not – of course, we ask to call the contact person to the phone), explain who you are, for example: "*Hello, my name is Diaz, from the "dso5.ru" company, we were talking with you about...*"

Remind the person where you've met and what you've agreed about ("we agreed to phone", "I received your contacts from..." etc.).

Our task is to give him a specific description of the previous meeting, a kind of a "hook": mark your moral right to call.

If the call is on the recommendation - point it out, if the call is in the agreement, recall your previous conversation.

You shouldn't lie in any case. We explain the reason for the call to the man up to the moment when he says, "**I remember!**" Or, for cold calls: "**I understand, what do you want?**"

The next step is building a context of the call.

1. Potential interest.

We clarify, if people cooperate with new partners:

- "Are you considering the possibility of cooperation with new suppliers, if conditions are more favorable?"

We ask individual questions, and the one who asks the questions – controls the conversation!

- "Would you be interested in changing the supplier of pipes, if we have more favorable conditions?" or

- "Are you willing to increase sales, if we offer our assistance in this matter?" Etc.

The answer is that we are waiting for – "Yes, there is a potential interest". If the person says "no", it is better not to waste time and go to the new call.

2. Work in our field.

The essence of this stage is to simplify the communication and turn it so that you have the right to ask the expert questions.

You say the following sentence:

"Let us proceed as follows. I will ask a couple of questions on the products, to clarify details and not to overload you with unnecessary information, I will make a selection and offer you our options. You will look at them, think and if you accept our offer, we will cooperate. But if it doesn't suit you, do not worry".

Our goal is to indicate that we are on the same level with the client. Let them know, that if you don't come to an agreement on the terms of cooperation, this won't be terrible. And when you will come into this position, you can move on to the expert questions.

3. Expert questions.

This unit is the most important to the process of selling. Here we sell the fact, that our manager is an expert, and the he is very well aware of the entire question relevant to our products. It expression might look like this:

- "How old is your child? Not all our toys suitable for children up to 3 years".

- "Do you have one child? These toys may be needed his little brother too".

- "Does he like the toys with music? We have a few options, and now we will choose the one that suits you best!" etc.

The same should be done if a person calls you into the office. On the request to tell about the product, manager must take the initiative – start asking expert questions to identify your customers' needs.

Attention, mistake! Once a customer asked "How much?" the manager names the price and keeps silence, as if waiting for a client "fall off". This approach is wrong! After the announced price, you just need to ask another question to make him "swallow" it.

Customer: "How much?"

Manager: "5000 rubles. And, by the way, have you already made the measurements?"

How to say the price if there was no questions block?

It's simple – you need to name the range of prices, for example, *"our products are different in price, from $20 per square meter up to $500 per square meter, depending on your needs"*.

After that, gradually move to asking questions: *"Let me ask you a few questions to find out exactly what you need and what kind of laminate will meet your needs. After that, I'll make an offer. If it suits you – fine, if not – do not worry"*.

Of course, it's not possible to overview all the nuances on this topic – for more information, consult the "Cold calling techniques" by Steve Schiffman. It's very interesting work, based on actual statistics of the results of sales managers.

Convertor: seller - shop.

The man in your store meets customers and helps them to choose the desired item, or bears the administrative functions.

While in China, I've noticed a strange thing – if you come into the store, the seller starts following you, as if planning to steal a wallet from your pocket. In our country, it was like that just a few years ago, but now we have gone from "following" the customers to the greater freedom. And yet, for the Chinese, it's okay, but for Europeans it is unacceptable.

<u>It all depends on the market that you are more focused on.</u>

Now we'll talk about the European approach, the approach of the CIS countries, European countries and we'll take a quick glance on America. Just a quick glance, because America has used its own sales technology for a long time now. In the matter of working with clients, they are ahead of the rest again.

How does a typical salesperson look like in every store? In brand clothes, suit or shirt with a nametag, right? People are waiting for this man. The difference is in the quality of service.

First, when a person walks into a store and the seller meets him, he is entitled only to inform the customer, but shouldn't order or insist on purchase. For example, *"if you are looking for men's clothing, you want to go here, if women's – here. If you have any questions, I'll be here"*. From this point, according to the European approach to communication with the client, **the seller completely stays away from the buyer**.

If you open a store in Asia, where communication is constructed in exactly the opposite way – the seller starts to go after the man, like importunate fly. However, this is a topic for another conversation – let's go back to a more appropriate model for us.

The essence of the "free" approach is that when a man walked into your store, **he is potentially interested in choosing the product**. Let him look, but do not stop him from buying!

And when a person has a question: "what do I choose?" he begins to turn his head around in search of a consultant. And that's the moment our seller appears – neither before nor after.

His mission is to say a simple word, "Yes?" and the man will ask. If the client just turned his head, flexing his neck, the seller should retire with the words "I'm sorry, I thought you wanted to ask something".

Task of the seller in the case of buying clothes – in any way to get the customer in the fitting room, because "test drive" of the product increases the conversion dramatically. If a person starts to try on clothing, refuse to buy comes much more rarely. The same applies to other types of products.

If at some point the client starts to walk away from the purchase, and you have a reason to believe that he just doesn't have the money, do not waste your effort – after some time, he will still come for the products. The only way to get him to make a purchase is to offer him to issue the credit.

We can learn from Chinese sellers confirmation that the item selected by the customer is suitable. After trying on, several store employees will in one voice assure that this shirt is the best thing you've ever put in your life. By the way, this method works just fine, so take it to your niche!

Suggest goods at a promotional price, tell him about the special offers. If the man tells you that he had chosen an item, but will come for the purchase later – excellent! Do not miss the sale – take his contacts and "finish" him.

Even if the customer has already bought something, you always have the opportunity to make the additional sale: "Have you already seen this tie?" "this shirt is perfectly suitable for this jacket", etc. Perfectly, the seller should have at least a basic understanding of the style – his capability will further enhance the chances of a sale.

So, if you summarize the scheme of interaction with the client, it should be like this:

Met –> showed –> offered –> "test-drive" of the goods –> discount –> money –> additional sale –> farewell

Convertor: store - merchandising

Moving on to the next convertor – your store.

We have already talked about websites and online stores – now is the time to discuss the offline business: shopping mall, retail outlet or a tent at the market.

What is most important?

1. **Placing the goods on showcases**. In addition to the sign, which is made by the already known technology (see territory map, the stream of people), you should place the top-sales (bestsellers) in the store window – this is our front-end (see corresponding section).

Your goal is to attract customers, to tell them about available products, make your unique offer and formulate the difference from the competitors. You must tune the man on those goods that he buys from you!

2. **Advertising and promotion**. Place, in addition to the front-goods, your offers from the category of "buy 2 for the price of one" in the store window. For example, "half price on Victoria's Secrets underwear" or "cheap shirts".

As for me, I've been placing the shirts for $10, and "drove" the stream of people initially through a cheaper model.

You'll earn on the products that people will buy when they enter your store and spot your range of products, not on those offers you advertise.

3. **Placement of the goods or merchandising**. More details on this topic you should find in the specialized literature. I highly recommend reading the "Retail Store" book, and yet I'll tell about the basic fundamental things you need to know and use.

The purpose of your work is to arrange items, so that people passing through the conceived path would take it and went to try it on. That is, your aim is not so much "sell now", but "trying on".

Why? As I have said, to "close" the deal after fitting is easier – conversion in this case is always much higher.

The client's path – from the entrance to the store to the exit point. Service, product, fitting, sellers – all those things are the parts of the road.

Be sure to consider the following question – "Which path should the client go to take the maximum number of items?"

A striking example of the successful organization of a "logistics" – the "Zara" shops network. Typical features:

- Fitting rooms are in the opposite side from the checkout;

- If the buyer has tried on a thing and he liked it, he goes to the cashier, picking up some things as he walks;

- There are small little things that contribute to the overall set at the checkout;

- Products are beautifully packaged, conveniently located.

People buy with their eyes. They judge not how clothing looks on them, but the way it looks on the mannequins.

<u>Clients buy an IMAGE!</u>

A few more points that you should pay attention to:

- Well-designed products on the showcase;

- Price-lists are all right (note if they are not spoiled and if they are large enough);

- Separation of male and female products on categories;

- Music assists the sale. While the client is going along the path made by you, it creates an "image" (remember the smell of coffee – it energizes you every morning and sells the cup itself). With a dynamic "without words" music it's easier for people to make a purchase. They're listening and not distracted by external factors, being in some kind of trance.

- The seller works in a store (see above).

- Put another poster at the exit of the store that says what discounts are at the available now – so that the person while leaving would see interesting information and leave his contacts.

Example: "You can get 500 rubles discount on your next purchase!" or "Leave your contacts and get a candy bar!" etc.

- Discount benefits regardless of whether the customer bought the product or not – because we, in fact, buy customers' contacts.

- Lack of excess of goods on the store window. Often stores hang on the set of goods on the limited area. It "compresses" them and so it is very uncomfortable to get things to try on. For high-quality sales, it is effective to reduce the range and focus on your niche.

All of these are the basic tips. In each case, there is quite a lot of details and additional information. Read, think, implement!

Convertor: shop - price tag

Another point on which I want you to focus right now – the tags that hang on your product.

When a person buys a shirt, it should be clearly understood, where the price tag is and what is written on it. The following must be present:

• Large font of prices, so that person didn't have to look closer. Leave the little stickers with pen-written things for amateurs.

• Crossed out price. It will work as a sort of deadline – "I need to buy right now, while it's best offer".

• Basic specifications. If it's clothing, then specify the material, dimensional mesh and other characteristics.

• Emotional description. If in clothing stores it is less relevant, then in the gadget store or home appliances store it is a powerful marketing tool. If a person is looking for a refrigerator for the family that can "make the ice itself", and the price tag will have this note – you'll hit "the bull's eye" and this will greatly increase the chance of selling!

• Good appearance of the price tag. It's a little thing, which is often not being followed – but it greatly affects the level of sales (see "Broken windows theory"). If you come to the store and see the broken price tags, torn pieces of paper, grubby inscriptions, then you immediately extrapolate this on the whole store.

• Price tags should be printed. Wean writing by hand – your calligraphy is useless.

• We hang some action next to the price tags: "2 + 2 = 5", "1 +1 = 3", etc.

• On the tags or in the product description you explain the additional benefit, the cumulative bonus, etc.

• Comparison with the item analogue or offers from the competitors (see on bodybuilding.com)

• **Common sense. As you have realized, is not worth all this stuff into one price tag!**

Convertor – office

Why do you even need an office? I've been working without an office for a long time. Why? I've been saving – negotiated in the cafe, in the offices of my clients, etc. For my workers I rented the working places in co-working centers (less than 100-150 USD monthly, however, the result is proportionally worse).

As soon as I realized that my business needs image, causing more credibility and quality, streaming sales, then began to organize a meeting in my office for 5-7 customers every day. In this case, the office becomes a vital necessity – the outdoor negotiations take too much time.

Office. Which one to rent?

We start from the size for your purposes. If you are just getting started, it would be better to rent a small office – do not just rent a penthouse in the best business center in your city. Base on your REAL needs.

The best option is 2-3 square meters per person. Meeting room separated by a wall or partition. You do not need the personal office yet – it is a luxury, not a necessity.

To rent in the center or on the outskirts?

If the office is only for calling ("cold" calls – sales, appointments over the phone), then the second option is preferable. If the goal is the prestige, then you need to rent a space in the center.

As an option – you can rent an expensive office for one day (you can see here – regus.ru/regus.ua) to meet with important clients.

There are couple of ways you can rent the office without money. I did so a few times and these techniques proved to work very well.

Since you only need an office for negotiations, then use:

- Your suppliers office, companies that you order goods from;

- Office of your partners;

- Office of your friends.

Hang a sign with your company's logo and name as required – and that's it!

When I had my own investment company, I was gladly negotiating with larger clients ("Sortis", "GT trade") and used their offices, marketing and IT-resources.

Another option, which I have already mentioned – you can rent a place in a co-working center. This kind of space where people gather from different companies, different professions – often freelancers – and work together on their projects. Find out where is the co-working center in your town (Google can help you), rent the meeting room and get to work!

You can also rent the working spaces for employees. Some companies rent a table at their buildings, computer and telephone – optional. Put you salespeople there and get into fight!

There is a little trick with an office. When you start the negotiations in your office, offer people tea or coffee, and leave on the table the marketing kit (booklet with information, customers, case studies, reviews, etc.) for 10 minutes, so when you come back, you will have communication on a completely different level.

Some other quick useful nuances within this chapter:

• You can "close" the sale directly from the announcement boards.

• You can add things such as the time counter to completion of an action to you Landing;

• Counter of increasing prices – "price increases right now, every minute you're missing all the great benefits!";

• Landing can be made through a special website lpgenerator.ru;

• The "Order a callback" button MUST ALWAYS BE on you website!

Conclusions:

• Your site serves only one purpose – to increase sales.

- In order to find a common language with the programmers and designers use templates created in special programs.

- Landing is an effective tool for collecting applications and making sales.

- Structures of Landing, an online store and selling the group in social networks are similar.

- Keep an eye on the work of your managers!

- Everything is important – from the design of price tags to renting location of your office.

Tasks:

- Draw your own templates for the website in the «Balsamiq».

- Think of examples of stores in the social networks.

- Measure the conversion of each component of the business.

- Rent an office for free, if you need it, of course.

- Turn on your main convertors – whether it would be the store, the seller, or something else.

Chapter 8: The average check

Average check – is the amount that the average customer spends per visit to your store. This indicator is calculated as:

Average check sum = (number of purchases / total value of purchases)

What now will be discussed? The fact that when a person comes to you, he buys the goods, for example, with an average value of $200. How can you increase that sum, which "tricks" you can use? What is the original price should be set for your services or products in order to earn more?

We'll talk about how to do it right in this chapter. I'll give you a few basic "tips" that can be implemented immediately – not to bother you with what you haven't yet encountered. There are many tools for solving such problems, but not all of them can be used from the very beginning.

How to set the price?

The first question that was interesting for me myself – what price to put on your products and services?

PRICE of good = Value + cost of good

If you put a price greater than that which is acceptable for the customers, their number decreases. If the price is not high enough, we will lose most of the profits.

The usual working scheme is to look at the prices on the market and to set the average of those. The problem is that this method does not resolve the dilemma mentioned above.

However, there are a couple of recommendations to help you determine the appropriate level of prices.

The first one is a niche. Are you working in a specific niche or selling everything to everybody?

If you were preforming the tasks of the previous stages, then you already have your own niche – not a lot of competitors and the product is in demand. Consequently, the price can be set much higher.

Niche stores always sell more expensive. This means that a store specializing exclusively in men's shirts, sells them more expensive than the store, which sells the entire range of men's clothing – shirts, pants, suits, ties, etc. Although the men's shirts can be the same.

The presence of niche enables to raise the price – plus you get the reduced costs of logistics and warehousing.

The second standard, which we take into account when setting prices – how full is the market and how many competitors are on it. If the market is filled with a large number of players, you cannot greatly inflate the cost of goods.

The same situation occurs when you are dealing with professional customers who are well aware in the niche.

Roughly speaking, if you sell bread or plates in bulk - raising the price of these commodities won't work: most likely buyers know their real market price.

I recommend adding 5-10% to the market price and supporting the value of goods with other properties: delivery, preferential conditions, etc. If your client is a professional and knows what the real price of this product is, you increase the average market price by 10%.

How to build the product matrix - Up / Down / Cross Sales.

From the previous chapters, we've already figured out what are the fronted and backend. Now it's time to make your product matrix, build a range of goods so we could get as much profit as we can.

This chapter describes one of the raising the average check technologies.

What is a product matrix?

Product matrix is a range of goods, which is divided into 4 types.

The first type is a frontend, "products-locomotives", and the products that you advertise. These are discounted products, goods on which you hardly earn, but use to attract customers.

The second type is a goods for Up Sale, goods of additional sale. This is a product, which goes on top of the main purchase – accessories, etc. The products that add value.

If you buy a laptop, the additional items could be the laptop bag, the keypad, or mouse pad. If you sell dances, the role of the Up Sale would go to the clothing, water, shakers, and sports nutrition. If shirt – cufflinks and ties would fit.

The third component of the product matrix is a Cross Sale, or analogue products. Thanks to them, you give the person a choice. These are products in the same price category – market "infantry", the main bulk of the goods.

If you sell DVRs for $ 500, the ones for $ 400 and $ 600 should stand next to those, so that the person had a choice – and you, if anything happens, could move to the sale of another product. It also includes the substitute goods (watermelon - melon, mp3-player - iPod, "Lenovo" laptop - "Samsung" laptop, etc.)

The fourth category includes the backend products. They are the ones we make the most money on. They are sold at high prices, if you have an average price of $ 500, the product of this category should have a price of 1000-2000 dollars.

This way you also create the respectable image: you are not just a store, you are the expensive boutique with all the ensuing consequences for the wallet.

<u>This kind of goods is not obliged to be sold. It is designed to support the sale of cheaper products.</u>

The striking example would be the coffee shops – they offer the small coffee, the medium coffee and the large coffee. What kind of coffee would you choose? Medium? Often people choose exactly it.

What happens if we remove a small coffee from the menu, thereby leaving the medium, large and extra-large? Now the choice falls on the large coffee, and so your profit also rises.

Up / Down / Cross Sale.

We have the technology of raising the average check using Up-, Down- and Cross Sale, based on the product matrix.

How to raise the average check by using the Up Sale? Once the person bought the goods from you, as soon as he made the decision and paid, it's time to offer him something "on top".

For example, a person bought a season ticket to the dance studio, and I invite him to buy a dancing clothing or a special sports nutrition, to make classes more effective.

How to raise the average check using the Cross Sale? If the customer says, "No, I do not need this ticket, this dancing style is not interesting for me", I am doing the offer of different style right away. There is a chance that he will accept. Not 100% of course, but there is a chance that he may be interested. Why not to use it?

How to raise the average check using the Down Sale? At the moment when a man tired of sale, will tell you: "No, I do not want it!" you still have a chance. Offer him a prototype or a mini-version, or goods of the lowest price possible (we are not talking about discounts here).

We're talking about a product, which costs lower initially. For example, if the person did not buy the training, you should be able to sell a book on the topic of the training.

A certain percentage of customers would "fall off", a certain percentage of people would agree. Your salesperson must sell each time during each contact with the customer!

In the online stores you should do like this:

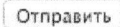

С этой книгой хорошо покупать

18 минут. Как повысить концентрацию, перестать отвлекаться и сделать де

(Экономьте 15.89 грн на следующей покупке)

And like this:

дистрибьютор: ООО "Электроник Артс"

Что делать, если программа не запускается

Рекомендуем также

ss Effect 2	Mass Effect 3	Dragon Age: Начало	The Elder Scrolls V: Skyrim
299 руб.	149,50 руб.	149,50 руб.	399 руб.
Скачать	Скачать	Скачать	В корзину

Work by the "steps": bought – Up Sale, didn't – Cross Sale, not at all – Down Sale.

Nobody gets out of here alive (c)

Announced bonuses. Sales magnets.

The next technology is announced bonuses.

We are creating a kind of "ladder" of indicators with price "steps" and bonuses attached to them.

For example, a customer came to buy a shirt and so he could potentially buy several things at once. Our task, as the seller, is to offer him something like this:

"Shirt that you want to buy is $49. But if you make a purchase of $100 total in our store, we organize either free delivery or you will receive a tie and cufflinks as a gift.

If you make a purchase of $ 250, you get two shirts on your choice as a gift! If the price of your purchase exceeds $ 1,000, you get..." etc.

We've put the sales magnets at $100, $250 and $1,000 – the person has to buy goods on the total sum indicated above, and then he will get a bonus.

You have to build a bonus system in steps. The first stage is $100, the second stage – $300, etc. We are attracting people to buy more and more like a magnet. The main thing is to tell the customers their potential opportunities, so that people were aware of the bonuses!

How do you know on what sums to put a "step"?

Analyze your sales. You will see that the majority of customers "stuck" at a certain mark and you should "push it up" as high as possible. For example, for shirts this mark was the sum of $70 in my experience. Accordingly, I pulled it up to the level of $150, then $250, and then $ 1,000.

Bundles (sets).

In order to make you sell your products successfully and increase their turnover in the warehouse, use bundles (sets).

If the shirt is worth $25, then the "buy a shirt, tie and pants for as low as $ 69" offer – is not nothing but a bundle.

Open the menu of any institution – there are so many of these proposals (tea, coffee + croissant, cheese soup + salad, etc.). Most interesting is that in many restaurants sets are more expensive than the same dishes separately.

People are used to that, if we are talking about a special offer, the product should be cheaper. In practice, this is not always true. You can pick up the price tag by 5-7% and people will not even pay attention to the price change.

Bundles are formed in such a way that they had one item on which you earn a lot, one frontend to attract the attention and the third item – addition, a link between them. Typically, the set consists of 2-3 items, but you can include a greater number of positions.

It works great at the online sports nutrition store bodybuilding.com: "We have gathered you the complete set on the "turnkey" basis, a discount of 30-40% and a list of 7-10 items, buy it!"

How to control the average check.

The question arises – how to control the average check? As you have realized, to measure the indexes is your duty. Do it!

Take the total sum of checks and divide by the quantity:

For example, 500 000 rubles per month, divide by 50 transactions, so it turns out that every customer makes purchases for an average of 10 000 rubles.

Tracks the cost of the average check dynamic – so you'll be aware of the financial position of your business.

Conclusions:

• When you set the price, take into account the availability of the niche.

• Use every way to increase the average check.

• Build your bonus system in steps.

• Bundles will increase the turnover of your products in stock and increase profitability.

• If you have a special offer, you can safely raise the average price by 5-10% – people won't even notice it.

• Continuously measure the values of your average check!

Chapter 9. Clients

Once we have assembled the product matrix, lets smoothly move one to the clients themselves – the circulatory system of your business. In this chapter, we will look at different types of customers, and you will learn how they can be classified and how to work with each of those.

We'll also talk about how to find the first customers, what the map of the territory is, what the client database is and how to effectively replenish it. As a result, we'll answer the question – how to make people buy from you again and again?

Four types of clients

In foreign marketing, they distinguish four types of customers for the main reason of purchase. You should focus on one or two categories; you will still "catch" the rest by following the recommendations. The question will be only one – who's more?

For each group of clients, the purchase decision is subject to certain criteria. For example, when purchasing windows, doors, often we will look for a low price, think about some of the benefits, the ratio of "price-quality". When buying luxury items, the price will most likely not be a major factor. When choosing a hair stylist, it is the "price-quality" that will be an important indicator.

So, **the first type of customers** – the people who are looking for the lowest price, the so-called **"freeloaders"**.

Their priority is the low price.

This type of client collects market information about where you can purchase this particular item cheaper. He compares the prices and buys the cheapest product – not always objectively beneficial, but it is always cheaper, even for a couple of cents.

This is the largest category of buyers, especially in the CIS – easy to work with by maneuvering the price, especially from the perspective of discounts.

The only nuance: cannot completely "submerge" into this category. Policy of reducing prices, regular discounts – the dead end, there is always a competitor, willing to work with a smaller profit. In addition, if you lower the price to a minimum, you're not earning anything.

Four types of clients – "Middleman" - professional

These people are looking for the greatest benefit at a reasonable price.

Priority – the "price / quality".

They pick up the goods of the best value – both for themselves and for their companies.

For example, all men become professionals when buying a car. They are trying to establish the value of the model, watch spare parts availability, reviews from the dealerships, etc.

Buying louvers, I was looking for not only the best price, but also specified who and how would install them, how it will happen, who will do the delivery, how much it costs. I was studying this question for a long time, called different companies, but compared not the prices, but a set of important factors for me.

This category yet knows what it wants, it is aware of the opportunities and standards available on the market. They choose for themselves the best conditions, but not in terms of price, but in terms of proposition value.

This category can be influenced only with better conditions than those that competitors have, - for example, "delivery to the door", execution time, better quality of services.

Four types of clients – "Urgent"

This type of customer is very common – they need something now, urgently, as they say, "yesterday".

Often, these are people who just forgot to buy something or to use your service – or they have a spontaneous desire to make a purchase. Such customers are willing to pay.

Example from personal experience: people, who were looking for a suitable shirt, came to me, but the right size was arriving in a week. Instead, I offered them the urgent delivery with a big price tag.

With this type of client, you have to correctly select the conditions of supply and delivery. And do not forget about your bonus for urgency! Take more money from them – it is permissible.

Four types of clients - VIP

The fourth type of customer is "luxury" or VIP-client. These people are looking for exclusivity, it is important to stand out from the gray mass. VIP-clients cover the minimum percentage of the audience.

The price is not important for these people – it is important to get the exclusivity, quality, they need something that does not exist elsewhere. For them, you can create the best value, make your exclusive offer.

9.5 One-time / regular customers

The next thing you should do is to determine what kind of business you will have – one-time purchases or loyal customers business. These are two completely different categories, which I mentioned earlier.

What is the difference between them?

When you have the business of one-time purchases you don't invest in service, do not develop your staff, but try to ensure that customers come and buy right now, bringing more money with every purchase.

The second option - you invest in something else: in service, in a loyalty program, discount cards, etc. In this case, your goal is to have a large number of regular customers, people that would come back again and again. From this viewpoint, the profit will be less but the stream of customers becomes more stable.

However, do not go to extremes. One-time purchase business is not always negative, roguery. For example, sellers of windows are often owners of one-time purchases business – people do not buy windows more often than once in 10 years. Accordingly, for this one-time purchase the want to sell as much as possible.

But even in this case it is possible to build a business model based on regular purchases. For example, automakers have noticed that people buy cars for 5-10 years and then are looking at a more expensive model. Then you can safely "invest" in them so the buyer will buy a car of the same brand, but more expensive in the future.

If you're into one-time purchases, you always have the option to save your customer database and sell them your new products or goods that were taken for the implementation from the partners.

The Matrix of customers

Over time, you collect the client database – and that means it's time to make your own matrix of clients. Earlier, we compiled the product matrix: customers matrix is constructed similarly.

To get started, open your database. No matter where you have it: in Excel, CRM, or just in a notebook - now we are going to highlight the categories of your customers.

The first category is 10-20% of people who spend the least money on the purchase. These are the clients on the attraction and retention of which we spend money, but they bring the least profits – often creating maximum amount of problems. Purchases are made rarely and their sum is small too.

Accordingly, we will invest less effort as well as money in the development and maintenance of activity of this category.

Note in your database in front of these clients: "call less often", "spend less money", etc.

The second category – the "middlemen", the main part of your customer base. We look at their numbers, who, how and what are they buying. For them, it is already possible to come up with special conditions, loyalty programs, "ladder of progress", etc.

With them you can already use the "standards" – call, offer and sell, not particularly going into every situation, but investing a little time and effort.

And **the third category** is 20% of customers. Those people who make a major profit. These are the VIP-clients.

Percentage of them is minimal in the database, but it is they, who bring the greatest profits. Remember the Pareto rule – 80 percent of the profits are gained from the 20 percent of customers. These may be people who buy annual subscriptions, passes, sets of clothes or make the bulk purchases.

There are not many of them, and you need to work with them in private, considering each situation individually and ensure that they won't leave you.

With these clients you can maintain communication in person – call, make special offers, adjusted your conditions of service for some of them.

Regardless of your product, you will have approximately same percentage of customer categories.

Customer database.

This is a kind of a document, the template in which you should always have marked: the client's name, age, phone, e-mail, date of birth, and basic information about him – all the things that you could learn. Also, be sure to monitor the whole history of shopping!

I'll be honest – it's boring to do that, for you and I, and other businessmen.

But, nevertheless, it is needed. What for?

• Phones and contacts – to sell products personally, to present new discounts, purchases.

• Name – for personal communication (you feel good as well when someone's referring to you by name).

• Birthday – to congratulate the client personally, give him gifts, give discounts on the birthday and motivate for new purchases.

• Purchase history – for the analysis of products, the demand for them. What product category does the client buy and what else he can buy additionally?

Where to have you customer database? At the start, use the standard tools – "Excel" or "Google Doc" tables. Subsequently, as appropriate, you can implement your own CRM system.

As an option – add customers through such websites as: smart-responder, just click, maichip.com etc. On these sites you'll be able to input the customer data, and immediately start sending emails. Moreover, you can add clients to this customer base directly from the site – just login and have a look, nothing complicated.

Once income is sufficient, I recommend setting up a CRM (system of customer relationship management) accordingly to your goals and needs. At first, I used "Excel", CRM-system I've implemented later. If interested, text me and I'll give you the contacts of an expert who can professionally help with configuration and start-up.

The first customers.

How to find the first customers, and where do we even look for them?

For example, you've started your business – now you need to get your first money. As I've said earlier, your friends, acquaintances and colleagues become you first source of money. These are the people who are in your circle of friends and trust, people whom you can call yourself.

How to find them?

You can pick up, ring up your phone book, and talk about what you're doing. Find out if they have any friends who need your products and services.

For example – *"Are you generally interested in this offer? Do you know someone who would be interested in it?"*

Bosses can be the second source of orders – if you meet the needs of the company, which you work in. This is a very big resource – you are being trusted in the company, and starting your own business, you are helping someone who you trust and hired you.

With the help of a larger partner, your business will develop faster. Boss – already a successful businessman, who can share with you his invaluable experience – especially if you're a good, sensible expert working for the benefit of his company.

The next searching area – your "neighbors", companies located nearby. If you couldn't establish contact with them, open the territory map (see in the next section), and easy work with it. In addition, you can always go back to the chapter on advertising and use a couple of free ways to attract customers.

Map of the territory.

Universal tool for work in your area. To make it, you will need a Google or another search engine, where there is a map of places around you.

Print it so that you see 5-6 blocks in the district and go round them all. On this map, you highlight all the companies, the entire key places where people gather, and the density of traffic on the streets. Note the estimated number of people attending this or that company every day.

Why do you need it?

You can conclude partnership contract with "neighbors" and advertise on their territory or for the interest or providing services – you need to think about what benefits you can provide to future partners.

Highlight the crowded places – where they move, where they live. We find the streets, which the majority of people go through – we also need to work with those: hand out flyers, place outdoors advertising (see previous chapters). Write down all the gathered information!

Cold and warm customers

What are these categories and how to differentiate them?

Perhaps you've heard of these two terms: "cold" client and "warm" client. Let me explain you what they mean.

Cold customer – is the one that hasn't bought anything from you, hears about you for the first time, and doesn't show any signs of interest.

For example, if you have a clothing store, the "cold" customers would be those who entered it for the first time and haven't bought anything from you yet. If you have a sales office, it will be those people who you're calling to with an offer of goods or services ("cold" phone calls).

Over time, the client shows the potential interest in becoming more "warm". For example, if I sell a shirt, the "cold" the customer is the one who just came to see the goods, and the "warm" will be the one who started to choose items to buy or tried those on.

If you have a sales business, the "cold" customers will be the ones who you ring up for the first time. The "warmer" customer is the one who showed interest in the proposal, and you call him again.

And finally, the "hot" customers are those who need a product right now. This client is willing to pay you the money, already knows all the terms and agrees with them. Accordingly, these people are quickly and easy to sell to.

If you feel difficult to close the sale with a "cold" calls, use the chain of 2-3 "touches" (call, an email, sending direct mail), with which you will increase the value of your offer and "warm up" the client.

In the online sales, for this purpose direct mail, mailing and messages to mobile phones are used. If you have a sales office, you can use the additional meetings, detours. Are you providing services? Implement the "test drive" – it was proved to be very efficient: clients are willing to use a free trial services.

Attracting clients on a long-term basis.

How to make the client come back and buy from you again and again?

It's very simple. The main thing – after the first purchase you give **a hook** to the client, which is to give him the cause to come back and buy from you again.

Customers come back to us when we exceed their expectations. Each person has his own expectations about level of service, level of product requirements. For example, he requires being treated well, wants to leave happy after the purchase, wants service of good quality and in time delivery of ordered goods.

Basic ways of attracting customers

The first way is **raising the value of the goods with bonuses**, thanks to the proposed additional benefits.

For example, in the coffee shops they give a flyer for a free cup of coffee, if you're making the second purchase. As for me, I use to give a discount on the next pass, which was valid for a period of 2-3 days with the purchase of the training in the dance studio.

The second way is a way of **improving the quality of service**. This method is not easy, but useful and aimed at the long term. Among the minuses we can mention the greater staff costs and, as a consequence, a smaller profit – but the high level of service will keep a lot of your customers loyal.

The third way is **specific conditions**. For example, long lines (the feeling of high demand and hype – McDonald keeps it at the proper level), and other unusual events and creative bonuses – invent you own tricks.

Loyalty Program

It is also called the discount system – when you give the customer the memory discount. The offer might look like this: "When you buy from us you get the VIP customer's card! Your discount is being summed up on it".

The introduction of such a system is a great tool for business development. The more customers buys, the more he becomes loyal to you because of the discount, and the more profit he brings.

You definitely need to make discounts "your people" to encourage those who are loyal to you. Develop your own discount system!

Many cafes, especially at the beginning of the way, underestimate this technique – they SELL these cards. Just think of it! They charge clients for it, thereby pushing them away and giving up the unique opportunity to get their contacts!

If finances do not allow you to release the card, then you can implement your discount system using the business cards – just print the current discount on it. When a person buys with it, you take it away from him and give the next one, which has a higher percentage of discount, etc.

Trust

Your main approach should be gaining and maintaining the trust of the customer to your business, your store.

Bear in mind – the older the person, the more conservative he gets. If young people like to buy from new companies and pay attention to innovation, the older generation prefers to be served by one company, with which relations have already been established. If they used to drinking "Coca-Cola", they will continue to drink it – in contrast to young people who do not have established preferences.

Aftertaste and the "WOW-effect"

Now we will talk about how you can make the "aftertaste" of the purchase as pleasant as possible for the client.

The first thing you can do is calling the customer and find out how is he doing using your item, is everything good, is he satisfied? So you will get a feedback on the purchase made in your store.

Better let the customer complain to you than to a friend!

If a customer is unsatisfied with anything, you can offer him a replacement, promotions product, bonus or a discount on his next purchase (the best option), to make compensation. Otherwise, the customer will be unsatisfied and most likely will not be back for the second time.

We can also discover who needs this kind of product among the friends of the customer and ask to recommend your company. As an option – ask for contacts and recommendations in order to call them on your own.

In order to make the customers come by themselves, and then bring their friends and partners, it is necessary to come up with some activities to encourage them – create the so-called "WOW-effects".

We can come up with a "thing" that will strongly encourage the spread of positive information about our company.

If we talk about dancing, it can be the flash-mobs, events, and foreigners' workshops. In regular store you can do something like this: Sasha Crazy* from Moscow, for example, came up with the following: "when making a purchase of some certain sum of money, saleswomen kiss at the checkout". Yeah! That's a wow effect!

Some implement the sales roulette, lotteries, some pranks: "spin the wheel and you'll see your bonus", "guess the number and get a discount", "pull the card – get a discount". Eagerness has a huge impact on the buyer!

For example, you can arrange "roulette" – if you can guess the number, the money paid for the purchase shall completely refunded – instead of giving the 3% discount! There's a plenty of space for creativity – invent your own "thing"!

Wow-effects are techniques related to sales that cause an emotional reaction. In Japanese cuisine restaurant waiter pours the tea from the half a meter distance or cooking right in front of you. In China, you have a pot of boiling water on the table, and you throw the ingredients for the soup by yourself, etc.

The clients, who will talk about you, remember his emotional state and will buy from you again and again, while taking a few friends.

Conclusions:

- There are four types of clients, each of which is focused on his own values when making a purchasing decision.
- To make the right decisions you should be regularly compile and analyze the matrix of clients.
- 20% of customers generate 80% of the profits – the law of Pareto.
- Maintaining the customer database is a necessary duty!
- Look in your notebook for the first customers.
- You must use all the ways to increase the average check.
- Wow-effect is the best way to make them talk about your company.

Tasks:

- Think of the wow-effect for your business.
- Create a loyalty program – at least with your business cards.
- Turn on the frontend / backend products.
- Start calling and wonder about customers experience after purchasing your product.

Chapter 10. Automation of business

<u>This chapter should be read only after the completing the previous tasks, otherwise, you just won't realize what is at stake, and won't be able to implement the techniques described below.</u>

In this chapter I'll show you how to run your business using the "autopilot", how to free yourself from your everyday routines and get the most free time.

We shall deal with a basic understanding of how the sales automation works. Here we'll take a little look on the bookkeeping, talk about SRM systems, recall the scripts and the bureaucracy questions once again, talk about issues of financial management. Also, I'll tell you about my own invention – united coefficient management system.

I ~~stole~~ borrowed it from McDonalds and remade by myself – you'll get recommendations about adaptation to a given model of management.

I hope that you'll perform all the tasks in the chapters, and now you already have a basic business, which can effectively develop and improve. Now it's time for the automation tools – you should agree that it's nice to realize that you are able to take a vacation at any time and at the same time you can successfully manage your business!

Types of business processes

There are two types of business processes:

Core – the key process which leads to the profit generation, it is the essence of business: making money. Here we include only the sales process, which directly affects the profitability of your business.

Additions to this process are the **sub-processes**. They help to work effectively, manage and sell more. It can be advertising, marketing, supply, logistics, etc. – the processes for the normal operation of businesses that require financial expenditures.

You need to understand that the first in line for development should always be the core business process – the sale. Answer the question – what makes money in your business, and what sub-units spend them?

The structure of business processes

Business process it's the operation. Realizing it, we can start writing job descriptions, handbooks for employee, and the seller, which will explain how to perform the operation, what the employee should do and how to control the process.

When you gather a folder of such instructions, the new employee will always find the answer to his questions in these documents.

The structure of a business process consists of such things as:

- **The Enter**. What do you need to do to get the business process started? For example, there was an incoming call or a customer walked into the store, or the application has come to your email.

- **The exit**. Exit point. How do we understand that the process is completed?

For example, when we get the money from the customer, the customer receives the goods, etc. If we receive the call, the exit is the end of the conversation.

- **The operation**. What exactly should I do?

How and what does the person say, if we are talking about a phone call?

For example: - **the enter** - the phone rang, **the exit** - put down the phone. **The operation** - script "hello, … company welcomes you! - I want to buy goods. - What exactly?" etc.

- **The goal**. What is the goal we are pursuing?

Sale of goods or the meeting appointment. It is important to make your employee (and customer too) understand why this process is even going on. What goal should we devote the operation to?

For example, if a person says, "Yes", then we pass him to the sales department, if he says "No", then we take his contacts.

Actually, we answer the question: "What kind of result is acceptable for us?" and describe the possible events.

The less your seller will think, and the more he will follow such instructions, the fewer mistakes will occur due to the "human factor". I'm talking about the routine, systematic work, which needs low-skilled labor.

In bureaucracy scripts help to reduce the risk of error, reduce the loss of service quality. If you hire top managers or highly qualified specialists, then they will need these scripts for management.

Accounting

I support as much automation of business as possible. So it happened, that I trust the machines more than people – and I would recommend you to adopt a similar approach to start a business. This will save you from many problems associated with incompetence and possible human mistakes.

This is especially important in such aspect as accounting.

I did my first accounting in "Excel". I've opened the file, inputted the data about earned money, counted income and expenses. If your income allows, I recommend giving accounting to professionals to free yourself from these responsibilities.

THAT'S IT! PROBLEMS WITH YOUR ACCOUNTING SOLVED!

Scripts and bureaucracy

You must have heard in movies such remarks as "damned bureaucrats" or the phrase "this bureaucracy shall end us all"? Well, often the majority of workers, thanks to the films, think just the same way.

What is bureaucracy for us, the managers?

The more accurately you will describe routine actions, the easier it will be to work for your employees – both experienced and beginners.

The most difficult and energy expending work is to make decisions. As soon as you will free yourself from the responsibility of constantly making routine decisions, you'll immediately feel the burden you've got rid of.

Admit it, rather than to explain each step to a beginner, it is easier to give him a pattern of actions that he will be able to learn and to act accordingly. In this case, everything is very much simplified from your part. But making a lot of explanations and scripts is not your task: to regulate their work is the problem of the workers themselves.

Do we need to regulate each action?

If the event is repeated 3 times, you should transfer it on the paper, write down the steps of what to do, how to solve the problem.

This is called "management by business processes automation" – so your employees will understand what they need to do, without requiring your participation.

"Semi-automatic"

Here I refer to scripts, checklists, sales books, brand books, inspections, etc. – everything that allows you to not take part in the routine work of the firm.

Let's take a closer look on a few things.

Check-lists

This is a list of mandatory actions that should be executed by an employee when he comes to the workplace.

Few years back, I was involved in the sale of trainings, consulting services, and I always had a paper on my table, on which was printed:

- Re-call 10 customers;

- Make 50 cold calls;

- Visit 2 companies;

- Smile to the customers, etc.

In this piece of paper, I've put the "done" mark after performing each task.

Your staff requires exactly the same paper, because they can simply forget to complete some task.

<u>We take away the right for ignorance from our workers</u>

Do the same for yourself – create your checklist to make sure your everyday necessary part of the work is done.

Control call.

It is done to check the quality of work of your employees – how the sale is performed in your company, is it easy to make a purchase for the customer?

I check my websites regularly, once a month, following my own instructions – to see how easy it is for me to pay for the dance class, how easy it is to find my website on the Internet. Using the same instructions, I ask people to buy a shirt, look how comfortable is it to choose the size, etc.

You can use the "mystery shopper" for the regular visits to your stores – after ordering something, the "client" comes, being serviced, and then he describes you all the faults of employees and the organization of work. This is very valuable information that you can productively work with.

http://4service-group.com/ – the mystery shopper website.

Automatic systems

Automatic control system (ACS) – is all the software and automation, including computers. ACS is something you can control, and that is not affected by the human factor.

For example, infrared sensors independently count the number of incoming people, checkout counts checks, biometrics – how much time your seller was actually working. Here we also include CRM, ERP-systems, contact databases, information bases, various counters – simply saying, everything that works "automatically".

I won't waste a lot of time talking about this topic – it's pretty simple, and information about buying and configuring ACS can be easily found on the Internet.

Financial Management

Foundation of financial management is your sales funnel.

It includes 5 indicators: "Lead gen" – generating new customers, the conversion – percentage of sales, the average check – the average sum spent by a customer in your store, the number of repeat purchases and margin.

Of these indicators a kind of conical "funnel" is being made: how many people know about you, how many of them come into your store, how many customers that came actually made a purchase, etc. Below I'll give you a list of nearly three dozen indicators – you'll choose only those indicators that are needed to control the situation and the development speed of your business.

After that, you must calculate the correlation and to estimate the united coefficient, the value of which reflects the general state of your business. In this case you can compare its value with a kind of "normative" level, beyond which it gives a very negative or super positive result.

For example, in "McDonalds" the final coefficient of key indicators is reduced to a value between 0 and 1. If it is equal to 1 – everything is good, if less – analysts study the indicators for the presence of "bottlenecks".

You can analyze the state of business with the help of those mentioned key indicators, including:

- The total enterprise value of you company right now, how much money you've invested in its development, what assets you have, what is their market price;

- Assets of the company per employee – what amount of assets do you have per one person.

- Income, expressed as a percentage of turnover: what percentage of the turnover is your profit.

- Profit as a percentage of the aggregate of your assets – how much profit brings each type of assets, what is the percentage.

- Return on net assets. Index, typical for larger companies. In your case it may indicate how much money the website gives you, how much money you invest in it, how much is returned to you in the form of profit.

- Return on total assets – how much money your hi-fi system brings you, and how much the sofa, etc.

- The total income in relation to total assets. This shows the effectiveness of the business.

- Profit before tax.

- Net profit after tax. These are two different indicators. Whether you need them or not – it's up to you.

- Profit as a percentage of total sales. Very important indicator!

- Profit per employee – how much money every person you hire brings you.

Personally, I always measure this indicator – it shows if some particular employee brings me profit.

"Value" of the employee doesn't end on the salary - add here the office rent, downtime costs, value of your time, training costs, costs in terms of missed

customers, receiving less profits, discounts, etc. As you can see, the price tag increases dramatically!

- Total income from new products;

- Total income from old products;

- Percentage of differences between them;

- Total income per employee;

- ROI – return on total assets, on invested capital, on investments;

- The marketing value added is the same.

- The percentage of growth, dividends, market value, the value of shares. These points, as well as the shareholders and their "turnover, are unnecessary for you right now – cross them out safely.

- The flow of money;

- Money in the bank;

- The flow of orders;

- What money do you have in cash;

- The flow of payment;

- The flow of goods;

- How fast the money comes on your account – the cycle of the transaction, how much comes per one cycle, and so on;

- Total costs, how much money do you spent;

- Receivables, what size is your debt, and how much you have to pay monthly for the service costs;

- The ratio of receivables to total assets;

- Income from interest of your own and issued as receivables funds;

- Average time of payment after delivery. This is also a very important point – how much time your client needs to pay for the goods. Personally, I measured this indicator constantly.

- Average time of money transfer after delivery. The same thing – when you'll get the real money.

- The average in-stock time of goods in warehouse. This will allow you to reduce the costs of purchasing, logistics, and expenses on warehouse.

- What is the percentage of loss in absolute figures during storage?

- What time percentage of workers' downtime? If your staff is not working, you're losing money.

Throw out all of the unnecessary indicators specifically for you, and measure required. After that, bring them into the united coefficient. Create your own "automatic", so the data would be entered without your participation, and calmly make your profit!

Conclusions:

- The core business process – sales, others only complement it.

- Make it so that your employees would think less – implement scripts and work algorithms.

- All accounting should be given to outsourcing!

- The first step to freedom is to free you from decisions on routine matters.

- Regular check of the company work quality – the guarantee of its development.

- Using a specified set of coefficients, you can monitor the results of your company down to the smallest details.

Tasks:

- Write down your core business processes – those that bring you money.

- Start delegate authority gradually, just partially at first, and then more and more.

- Calculate the profit from performing the tasks and text me on jtc.audit@gmail.com – and if you attach the review – I'll send the bonus course.

Afterword:

Five rules of successful business:

1. Find a partner – it takes at least two to become a champions.

2. Choose the date and time in the future, before which you will achieve success.

3. Calculate indicators of your business!

4. Change the atmosphere – it will help you to be distracted from the constant workload.

5. Write down your victories!

www.ingramcontent.com/pod-product-compliance
Lightning Source LLC
Chambersburg PA
CBHW072036190526
45165CB00017B/954